Praise for Synergy Team Power

"At Mercedes, we strive to give our customers the best service in the world. That is why we engaged Chris Alexander and his Synergy Team Power program to help us maintain our competitive advantage. Synergy has been a great success for us.

"Our customer satisfaction ratings rocketed! We now work more effectively as a team to satisfy our discerning and demanding customers."

-Bob Evans, Senior Service Manager, Fletcher Jones Mercedes Benz

"Chris Alexander helped us improve our business greatly. He helped structure our systems and processes, improve our customer service and in every aspect of our business, we became more Synergized and focused. He understood our creative approach and adapted his Synergy Team Power program to suit us–the results are absolutely outstanding!"

-Lisa Klang, President & C.E.O., Klang & Associates

"Chris Alexander and the Synergy Team Power Program have made us a better organization. The interactive and creative approach to improving our service and communication to our customers–both internal and external–and the overall team development have had a dramatic impact on our overall success. Chris has helped us instill a cultural change and philosophy that is needed in business today, one that is focused on service, communication, and teamwork regardless of the targeted customer. Thanks for playing a key role in our success."

-Scott Grugel, C.O.O., Interior Specialists, Inc.

"Wonderful! Brilliant! First thing was joy and effective immediate tools that lead to success. I cannot recommend Chris and his Synergy Team Power program highly enough!"

-Liz Jaeschke, Prescott Management

"Margaret Mead described you perfectly. It was Synergy in action! The words of wisdom and wit that were shared will live long in the hearts and minds of the students, teachers, and business people who attended.

"Thank you again for sharing your time and talent with FBLA. I really enjoyed the opportunity to work with you and hope that we can work together again soon to help build leaders of the future."

-Diane Yen, Future Business Leaders of America

Ignoring human synergy
is like tossing the pieces of
a puzzle on the floor and
expecting them to fit together
on their own accord!

The 5 Success Habits of High-Performance Business Teams

by Chris Alexander

Publisher: 1+1=3 Publishing
www.SynergyTeamPower.com
First Edition
Library of Congress Cataloging in Publication Data
Alexander, Chris
Synergy Team Power: The 5 Success Habits of High-Performance Business Teams
Includes biographical references and index.

Project credits:
Line and Final Editing: Sharon Young
Graphics: Shand Coetzee and Chris Alexander
Cover, Layout, and Design: Maryna Coetzee

Also by Chris Alexander:

Business Books, CDs, and DVDs:

Synergy Strategic Planning

The "WOW" Factor!

The "WOW" Factor! CD

The "WOW" Factor! DVD

Synergy Sales Power

Synergy Leadership

Joy in the Workplace

Joy in the Workplace, CD Album

Joy in the Workplace, DVD

Synergizing Your Business Handbook

Success Is Fun Audio Album

Synergizing Your Business Audio Album

Personal Development:

Creating Extraordinary Joy

Creating Extraordinary Joy, CD Album

Creating Extraordinary Joy, DVD

Synergy Life Mastery Audio Album

Catch the Wind with Your Wings

Synergy Team Power Credo

Synergy is a force multiplier that elevates morale, quality workmanship, and a sense of pride in accomplishment. It turns people around from fear motivation to desire motivation.

Synergy is optimistic and strives for excellence as a natural consequence of its meaning. It promotes unity, covers up triviality, and builds bridges instead of walls.

Synergy creates a sense of belonging and existentialism, which are the seeds of personal security. It devastates greed and eliminates destructive ego and introduces learning.

Synergy powers up innovation and stifles bureaucracy, and makes everyone say "us" instead of "us and them." Triple-win becomes a way of life where: the customer wins, the company wins, and the team wins . . . in that order.

Every goal, every function, and every success within an organization is much more gratifying and easily achieved . . . when there's Synergy. People multiply success when communicating and cooperating with one another . . . that's Synergy.

It is a force that can work for you . . . if you'll let it!

Contents

It's amazing what can be accomplished
when nobody cares who gets the credit."

-President Harry S. Truman

INTRODUCTION

Next fall, when you see geese flying south for the winter in a "V" formation, you might consider what science has discovered about why they fly that way.

As each bird flaps its wings, it creates an uplift for the bird immediately following. By flying in a "V" formation, a skein of geese adds at least 71% more flying range than if each bird flew on its own.

When a goose falls out of formation, it suddenly feels the drag and resistance of trying to go it alone, and quickly gets back in line to take advantage of the lifting power of the bird in front. When a head goose gets tired, it rotates back in the formation and another goose flies to point. Geese honk from behind to encourage those in front to keep up their speed.

When a sick or wounded goose falls out of formation, two other geese fall out with that goose and follow it down to provide help and protection. They stay with the fallen goose until it is able to fly, or until it dies. Only then do they once more take to the sky and fly at high speed to catch up with their teammates.

The geese instinctively create power to achieve their goals through the phenomenon of "Synergy." Synergy is the additional benefit and often invisible, mysterious advantage created by combined effort. We've all been touched by the power of teamwork at one time or another – Synergy in action, the result of combined energy creating something greater than the sum of its parts.

As with geese, business teams that share a common direction, a sense of purpose and commitment, will achieve extraordinary results faster and easier by traveling on the trust of one another. Teams who support one another with "honks of encouragement" and great attitudes, do their part and make work fun, creating an emotional and motivational glue that makes a job feel extra special and worthwhile.

Synergy Is the Secret

What are you looking for when you watch your favorite sports team? You want them to win. You want them to use the special talents of each player. You want each player to do his or her part! You want them to get in sync and do what they are supposed to do; and when you see that happening–your team working in harmony–it fires you up. It energizes you. It's exciting, it's fun, and it makes you want more.

In business, as with world-class sports teams, teamwork is a competitive advantage. If there are two companies competing for the same contract, the teamwork company will win every time. The track record of improved performance through teamwork is well documented.

NASA has been teaching astronauts to work in teams for years. Lockheed Martin, Northrup Grumman, and BAE Systems won a $200 billion F-35 Joint Strike Fighter contract by joining forces. Southwest Airlines, Google, Apple Computers, Xerox, FedEx, Levi Strauss, Boeing, and Harley Davidson are all teamwork companies. When a group of committed individuals comes together, united behind a common set of goals and core values, barriers are broken and magic's in the air. Your customers can sense it.

Working in today's world is different from the way it used to be. Society has changed a lot. Many of the traditional ways that generations before us could rely on have disappeared. Competition today is global; companies are bought and sold, and markets are tossed around radically by the winds of change. Through technology, we are now more connected than at any other time in our history. We have to shift the way we think and feel about the workplace. We need to adapt and make change a source of strength rather than a source of stress. We need to create our own certainty and balance–both of which are entirely within our control.

There is no difference between a high-performance business team and a team of Olympic athletes

When we practice Synergy in the workplace, we bring more balance into our lives. The bridges we build with others become our daily support system and help us feel more confident. Human connection is a primal need and when we connect with one another in positive ways and work together toward a shared destiny, we experience a deep and primal validation, and a sense of purpose. This results in an emotionally secure workplace: a place of safety, trust, balance, and certainty.

Synergy Is Shared Destiny

The *goal* of Synergy is the compounded mutually beneficial gain achieved from working together toward a shared destiny. The foundation of Synergy is relationship trust and the essence of Synergy is the inspiring shared experience. We can't truly share the experience if you're lifting and loading or blocking and tackling, while I watch. An equal input of energy is required for both of us to benefit. Team members must be competent at what they do and share in the lifting and loading. It's about working together willingly to make great things happen– taking the good with the bad. Like the Canadian geese when we travel on the thrust of one another and make sure team members have the chance to voice concerns, ideas, and suggestions, we arrive at a better destination faster and easier.

We don't have to do the same job, but there has to be equality in the effort we make. And if things go wrong–as they sometimes will–we share the embarrassment, the remedy, the rebuilding, and the eventual reward. Ideally, Synergy should start right at the beginning, with everyone involved in the mission, goal, or project. Teams should be in on the decision-making and planning, so there is shared emotional investment from the beginning. Synergy runs on energy, and the energy at the beginning of a project is extremely powerful and motivating. You want everyone in on it, and you want them to know what to do and be competent. A lack of competence will lead to a lack of trust, which will inhibit team Synergy.

For most of us, positive human interaction and recognition are major motivators. When we trust one another and our attitudes are positive, it's fun to come to work. The idea of helping others and working together willingly is easy. In this kind of environment, we give more of ourselves, without hesitation.

We are all in the energy business, and high productivity and extraordinary performance are directly connected to how team energy is directed. If team energy is directed toward a shared destiny, then job satisfaction, quality of work, accountability, and responsibility are all elevated, making "team player" one of the most sought-after work traits. This is verified by the results of a survey conducted by the well-respected research company, Challenger, Gray & Christmas, Inc.

In 125 companies in 34 industries, senior management ranked "team player" as their number one workplace value. Out of the top seven desirable work traits, over 50% of middle managers chose "team player" as the most important work trait, and the balance chose it as their second or third most important.

According to those surveyed, employees between the ages of 30 and 40 are most likely to possess the best teamwork attitudes and skills. The seven traits covered in this survey ranked as follows:

- ► Team player

- ► Self-starter

- ► Dependable

- ► Company-focused

- ► Responsible

- ► Adaptable

- ► Likeable

"Our Distrust Is Very Expensive."

-*Ralph Waldo Emerson*

Why I Wrote This Book

All over the world, there are individuals who want to go to work–who are excited to go in on Mondays. They love their jobs because the environment they work in is free of fear and emotional toxicity; and they are unimpeded and able to focus on their work. They do their part to help achieve organizational goals.

I work with people like this everyday, and I help them create the kind of workplace they have always wanted–one that delivers a sense of belonging, personal satisfaction, and job enrichment. I make this happen by working with business leaders who know that businesses and organizations are only as good as the people in them, and they recognize the importance of winning the hearts and minds of their people. I build high-performance teams: in businesses, government agencies, churches, non-profits, and even families. I have witnessed astounding personal, financial, and organizational growth accelerate when the environment is free of fear and supercharged with Synergy Team Power.

This book is for all employees–from entry level all the way up to the executive suite–who are looking for a way to create a meaningful workplace that delivers continuous job satisfaction. It demonstrates that adopting the value of teamwork and service, along with the importance of treating fellow workers with courtesy and respect–as one does with a customer–makes all the difference. You will find helpful stories, examples, anecdotes, and checklists that have grown out of many years of building and working with high-performance business teams. These stories are about real people who have found a way to create satisfying, fun jobs, and at the same time, build safe, secure, and highly-profitable work environments.

There are 5 Synergy Team Power success habits:

- ► Building Trust

- ► Right Mental Attitude (R.M.A.)

- ► Make It Fun

- ► Be a "First-Giver"

- ► Be a Synergist

Within each of the success habit chapters, I have sprinkled humorous and relevant examples, quotes, and anecdotes to make your reading experience pleasurable and meaningful. My vision is that you will find a special message that resonates with you on a personal and professional level, and that it helps you recognize the important role you and all of us play in creating emotionally secure, profitable work environments. My larger vision is that as more and more of us recognize the value of Synergy and its profound benefits, we will work together to expand its application to build stronger families, better schools, profitable businesses, safe cities, and peaceful nations.

High-performance business teams are comparable to high-performance sports teams. Like sports teams, business teams "want to" bring all their individual talent and abilities to work. They create a safe, secure, interpersonal environment; openly share ideas; and willingly focus their energy and efforts on a shared destiny.

Success Habit One: Building Trust

You can't order trust like you order a pizza. When you make pizza for a living, you quickly learn the "secrets of the trade." Once you see the benefits of doing it, you'll wonder why you didn't try it sooner.

The Courage to Trust

Do you want to do business with somebody you don't trust? Would you want a relationship with someone you don't trust? Of course you don't! Trust is the foundation for all good personal and work relationships. It satisfies an emotional appetite for true connection and unity, and it begins by trusting yourself first. When you trust yourself, it's easier to trust others. It takes courage to know who you are, to recognize your strengths and weaknesses, and still see the value of your contribution to yourself, others, and life.

In a scene from the romantic comedy "Moonstruck," a neglected housewife eats dinner with a man she meets at a restaurant.

Afterwards, he walks her home. When he realizes that the house is empty, he asks if he can come inside. He is handsome and charming, his intentions are clearly romantic, her husband is cheating on her, the house is empty, and she would never get caught if she said yes. But she says, "No," and when her chagrined suitor asks, "But why?" she answers, simply: "Because I know who I am."

The blandishments of a handsome man were mere distractions to this character: She would go on being who she was. And in this lighthearted movie, we have a statement that is not lighthearted, but is one of the most important lessons life can teach: You have to know who you are. You must have a good and trusting relationship with yourself.

When you know, really know, what matters to you, your actions mirror your beliefs. Your self-respect will not be swayed by external events. Other people may distress you, may even cause you harm, but you have something so solid to hold onto that you cannot be swayed into making foolish decisions, even attractively foolish decisions. There is a marvelous comfort in knowing who you are.

Victor Frankl, author of *Man's Search for Meaning,* found that "piece" of knowledge in the hellishness of a concentration camp. People who had every reason to believe in their imminent death found reasons to live, found ways to care for one another. In a situation designed to bring out the worst in humanity, they found the finest in themselves. These people, strong spirits in tortured bodies, put their energies into being good to one another. Their focus was outward, positive, and helpful. In the midst of a living nightmare, they still knew, or maybe knew even better, who they were.

Albert Einstein believed that human beings, to realize their potential, must have clear standards of right and wrong. The most important human endeavor, said the famous scientist, is striving for morality in our actions. "Morality is what gives beauty and dignity to life. Following our animal instincts is not enough. Without high standards of right and wrong, men cannot live together in peace and friendship."

In your personal and business life, trustworthiness is fostered and earned by honoring and paying your dues through diligent effort, quality work, and pride in accomplishment. It is going the extra mile and being loyal to yourself and the commitments you make to others. Being your own person is about being self-directed and authentic. It originates at our core by choosing to live and work by a set of ethical standards, beliefs, and values. Authenticity, transparency, and integrity are all from the same family and when service to one another is embraced as a value, trustworthiness is experienced, making it easier to make decisions and solve everyday problems. If you are not authentic and sincere, you will encourage mistrust, fear, and distance.

Integrity means not forsaking what's right for the approval and acceptance of any person or group. It means not engaging in unethical manipulation of others to do what's morally, legally, and humanely wrong. It's knowing that no right thing can come from wrong thinking.

Mark

Young Mark came from a good family. Trust was highly valued and Mark took pride in always trying to be honest. "Mark, Sr. loved his son and always impressed upon him to do the right and honorable thing regardless of the temptation. He would always say: "Son, your reputation and integrity are your most precious assets."

Today Mark would be tested. He could hear those words ringing in his ears as he stood facing the time clock. His own timecard in his left hand and Jason's in the right. Jason, a good friend and coworker, asked him to clock-in on his behalf. Jason was late. He knew this was dishonest and against company policy. Conflicted, angry, and confused, he was torn between right and wrong. Jason was his friend and he was tempted to do it. What would happen if he got caught? Would he lose his job? He despised these feelings and decided to put Jason's card back in its slot. "My reputation is all I have" he thought. "I like Jason but I'm not prepared to compromise my honesty."

When we are both trustworthy, we help each other achieve our highest potential, resulting in zones of inspiration and profitable work environments!

The Enemies of Trust

In Buddhism, one of the core doctrines is titled The Three Poisons. These are greed, hatred, and delusion. Besides the negative karmic effect of these three poisons, they also form the basis for a lack of trust and are the roots of dishonest thoughts. Greed of any sort, even greed of knowledge, diminishes your authenticity. You become unbalanced. Hatred brings about vengeful thoughts, which in turn lead to duality and dishonesty. Delusion, within itself, cannot be trusted. Many of our fears and paranoia stem from over active imaginations.

The way to be trusted and to trust others is to follow the Golden Rule: "In everything, do unto others as you would have them do unto you; for this is the law of the prophets." –Jesus of Nazareth.

False fronts and facades produce insincere energy transference. What we think affects how we feel, which plays out in our body language and nonverbal communication.

If someone is untrustworthy, their next consideration is power and control over others. If an untrustworthy person has power, the collapse of an organization is inevitable and employees, investors, and even industries get hurt.

The FBI continually conducts investigations into corporate fraud matters. The 2008 sub-prime lending crisis devastated individuals and companies and put the world economy into a tail spin. History has demonstrated that a workplace that is secretive and duplicitous can teach people to become untrustworthy; but if character is taught in childhood, it remains the same across most situations. Being trustworthy is demonstrated in one's behavior and actions. It is a state of one's character, and in the workplace character and trusting relationships are essential ingredients for long-term success.

If you hire for character and train for skills, you'll have a good chance of establishing a workplace filled with trustworthy people.

In the final analysis, trust is the most valuable asset we have. It is having the courage and inner strength to stay away from being deceitful, cheating, stealing, betraying, and speaking with a forked tongue. It is having an inner resolve that is based on respect and love for ourselves and others. Our behavior is the end result of what we believe to be the truth. If our truth is that we respect another person's property and life, we will not abuse, use, break, or consider taking them.

Hire for character and train for skills!

Building Trust

Courage of His Convictions

Abe Lincoln gave the greatest speech of his famous senatorial campaign at Springfield, Illinois. The convention before which he spoke consisted of a thousand delegates together with the crowd that had gathered with them.

His speech was carefully prepared. Every sentence was guarded and emphatic. It has since become famous as "The Divided House" speech.

Before entering the hall where it was to be delivered, he stepped into the office of his law-partner, Mr. Herndon, and, locking the door, so that their interview might be private, took his manuscript from his pocket, and read one of the opening sentences: "I believe this government cannot endure permanently, half slave and half free."

Mr. Herndon remarked that the sentiment was true, but suggested that it might not be good policy to utter it at that time.

Mr. Lincoln replied with great firmness: "No matter about the policy. It is true, and the nation is entitled to it. The proposition has been true for six thousand years, and I will deliver it as it is written."

-Good Stories for Great Holidays

TEAMWORK: Teamwork is the secret to success. When we treat each other as internal customers with dignity, respect, and efficiency, we create a culture of cooperative high-performance, which ripples out to the external customer.

RESPONSIBILITY: Take 100% responsibility for your role in the team; be highly competent, reliable, objective, and accountable. Good team players don't blame others and when they're wrong, they admit it quickly and learn from it.

UNDERSTANDING: Understand the differences in others; build bridges of cooperation, respect, and trust. Prejudice has no place in teamwork. We are uniquely different—races, religions, cultures, genders, beliefs, and abilities.

SEEK SYNERGY: Look for ways to work more harmoniously with your team to multiply efficiency and service to the customer. Synergy is all about creatively seeking ways that will multiply the quality of workmanship, relationships, and the excited feeling of achieving the extraordinary; that means that everyone on the team learns to play from the same sheet of music, secure within themselves and their own individual talent to contribute with no fear of loss.

TALK IT OUT: Honest relationships are vital to team success. An effective way to build trust and honest relationships is to deal with conflict immediately in an objective, constructive, and candid manner. The key is to avoid ego defensive comparisons. It is not "who" is right, but "what" is right. Focus on solving the problem, not each other.

A Credo for Relationships

I choose to trust myself, others, and life.

I choose to be authentic.

I choose to communicate in truth.

I choose to help not hurt.

I choose knowledge over ignorance.

I choose to listen more and talk less.

I choose peace over aggression.

I choose to respect and be respected.

I choose to give, rather than take.

I choose humbleness over arrogance.

I choose optimism over cynicism.

I choose love over fear.

Teamwork

Emotionally secure individuals make the best team players.

Secure competent individuals understand the power of teamwork. Secure individuals are comfortable with sharing information because they know that their creativity and growth come from sharing ideas.

Teamwork requires an understanding and an individual commitment to achieving goals together–a willing commitment to make things happen in concert with others. This makes teamwork difficult for insecure individuals who are afraid to share their knowledge or themselves with others.

Teamwork means using the strengths of each individual in brainstorming, planning, problem-solving, and allowing the experience and abilities of each team member to have a voice. Because it's exciting to be empowered, individuals are more willing to participate in creating solutions, setting goals, and executing them with a greater sense of urgency.

Making 1+1=3 . . . or more!

Working in teams means allowing a free flow of ideas, which opens the door to disagreement and debate. From time to time, working as a team will mean allowing the most qualified person to lead. Unlike cooperative groups, real business teams do not meet, just for the sake of meeting. Teams meet to share responsibility, share the load, find solutions to problems, and work out ways to be more effective. In a nutshell, teams meet to find more efficient ways to achieve goals that ripple out to manifest the organization's vision.

Teamwork focuses on directing individual creativity, energy, experience, and ability toward a shared destiny; and it requires a greater understanding of human behavior. Interpersonal communication must remain sensitive, pro-active, flexible and in some cases, tolerant of mood changes, circumstances, and different personalities. A good team will make their differences their strengths–as opposed to groups of people who will form cliques and fall into the trap of "group-think," seeing differences as incompatibility.

Supporting differences does not mean consensus and agreement just for the sake of harmony, or to create warm feelings amongst the team members–it means directing those differences as strengths toward goals in the same way you would with experience and skills. For example, motivated, talkative, social initiators may be difficult to handle in a team, but their strength in verbal communications and social situations would make them the most qualified to present ideas to larger meetings and upper management, thus bringing victory to the team. When you focus on the strengths of others, you build trust and respect. When you focus on the weaknesses of others, you foster conflict and distrust.

As with Olympic sports teams, good business teams are continuously looking for ways to improve their performances–by carefully examining how the last project was carried out and how the goal was or was not achieved and by asking the all important questions: "What could we do better?" and "What do we need to improve?" In this way, the team becomes comfortable with critical evaluation and measurement and through continuous improvement, more successful.

Synergy Is the Secret.

There are a number of extremely valuable strategic reasons why teamwork has been at the center of success for thousands of companies . . . large and small:

- ▶ Higher levels of productivity
- ▶ Higher levels of quality
- ▶ Higher levels of motivation
- ▶ Higher levels of customer satisfaction
- ▶ Higher levels of employee satisfaction
- ▶ Higher levels of belonging
- ▶ Higher levels of job satisfaction
- ▶ Higher levels of job enrichment
- ▶ Higher levels of communication
- ▶ Lower levels of attrition
- ▶ Lower levels of conflict
- ▶ Lower legal costs
- ▶ Lower stress related claims
- ▶ Lower absenteeism
- ▶ Low workplace hostility
- ▶ Lower costs of production
- ▶ Lower costs for loss control

Who Do You Thank?

Charles Plumb, a Navy pilot on his 70th mission, was shot down and unfortunately parachuted into enemy territory. He was captured and spent several years in an enemy prison. Upon his release along with many others, he was interviewed on national television and this led him to give lectures on the lessons he learned from his experience.

One day, some years later, a man approached him in a restaurant: "Are you Charles Plumb?"

"Yes–do I know you?" asked Plumb.

"Not directly," the man replied, "but I was the sailor who packed your parachute on your last mission."

Plumb, amazed and grateful, thanked the man. "If that chute didn't open, I wouldn't be here today."

"I was just doing my job as part of the team," the sailor replied.

Plumb realized that this sailor, like so many others, held the pilots' lives in their hands. They did it with diligence, commitment, and with great care. Because they were a part of a dedicated team, they never expected recognition.

"Who Packs Your Parachute?" Who helps you through life, physically, mentally, emotionally, and spiritually? Be grateful to them for doing their part and recognize them by saying "thank you"!

-Captain J. Charles Plumb

Responsibility

Be a part of the solution and not a part of the problem.

Response-ability: The ability to answer for one's conduct and obligations. To be accountable, to be trustworthy. A moral obligation to do one's duty.

Trustworthiness is established with internal and external customers by the level of responsibility shown to your job. If you say you are going to do something, you will be measured by your word and your responsiveness to execute precisely what you said you will do.

Trust compounds and grows every time you demonstrate your responsibility. Trust diminishes rapidly with unreliability. People unwittingly test one another on the principles and the values that sustain an ethical and moral society. Even dishonest people use these principles as measures of trust.

Teams must be responsible, reliable, and held accountable for their performance. Teams are not designed to be a forum for justification and excuses. If a goal has not been achieved, the first step is measurement and analysis to determine margins of error. Then the team can problem-solve to find solutions to reduce the margins of error and move forward with a re-implementation plan of the best alternatives.

Two Brothers and the Geese

Two sons work for their father on the family's farm. The younger brother had been given more responsibility and reward, and one day the older brother asked his father to explain why.

The father said, "First, go to the Kelly farm and see if they have any geese for sale–we need to add to our stock." The brother soon returned with an answer. "Yes, they have five geese to sell to us."

"Good," replied the father, "ask them the price." The son returned with the answer. "They are ten dollars each."

"Now ask if they can deliver tomorrow." On his return he answered, "Yes, they can."

The father asks the older brother to wait and listen, and then calls to the younger brother in a nearby field. "Go to the Davidson farm and see if they have any geese for sale–we need to add to our stock."

The younger brother soon returns with the answer. "Yes, they have five geese for ten dollars each, or ten geese for eight dollars each; and they can deliver them tomorrow. I asked them to deliver the five unless they heard otherwise from us in the next hour. And I agreed that if we want the extra five geese we could buy them at six dollars each."

The father turned to the older son, who nodded his head in appreciation. He now realized why his brother was given more responsibility and reward.

-Author Unknown

Understanding

When we focus on the strengths of others, we build trust and respect!

Everyone is an individual. In the workplace today, you will find people from different cultures, who think differently, have different values and rituals. In the United States, as with many countries around the world, an array of languages are spoken.

People from all over the world move to other countries to better their lives; therefore, culture shock is not uncommon. Many new immigrants find it difficult to adjust and connect with the new ways and let go of the old. People who are raised in different cultures are proud of their national heritage and go to great lengths to protect who they are, and that's a good thing. They draw a sense of emotional security from their frames of reference–how they were raised.

Fostering the Value of Understanding

It is tolerance and understanding of differences that allow different cultures, religions, genders, and opinions to work together in harmony. By choosing to foster tolerance and understanding, you multiply the potential to find different and new solutions to everyday problems. Fostering tolerance and understanding leads to focusing on the strengths of one another, which in turn builds trust and respect–the basis of all good relationships. For all nationalities, a good attitude is more acceptable because it can contribute to faster assimilation, connection, and personal security.

Fostering understanding will also open the door to similarities. People are people, and good interpersonal communication is appreciated around the world. We are similar in many ways–we all want to be respected, we all want to maintain our dignity, we all prefer positive communication. Observing different cultural rituals and demonstrating the willingness to build a bridge of communication, cooperation, and collaboration will, without a doubt, create reciprocal behavior.

10 Tips for Fostering Understanding

1. Look for ways to connect and Synergize. "It's you and me against the problem, not you and me against each other."

2. Be aware: Observe different cultures and foster understanding by sharing your differences and similarities.

3. Be careful not to overpower people by intimidating them with size, voice, and personal space.

4. Slow down, talk less, and listen actively.

5. Be sensitive to gender differences.

6. Criticize actions–not people, genders, or cultures.

7. Avoid power plays, stereotyping, sexual comments, and personal innuendoes and jokes.

8. Be polite, courteous, and respectful.

9. Smile and relax while communicating.

10. Be inclusive, ask questions, and invite opinions.

A person who doesn't stand
for something will fall for
anything.

The Blind Men and the Elephant

It was six men of Indostan
To learning much inclined,
Who went to see the Elephant
(Though all of them were blind),

The First approach'd the Elephant,
And happening to fall
"God bless me! but the Elephant
Is very like a wall!"

The Second, feeling of the tusk,
Cried, -"Ho! what have we here
This wonder of an Elephant
Is very like a spear!"

The Third approached the animal,
And happening the trunk to take
"I see," quoth he, "the Elephant
Is very like a snake!"

The Fourth reached out his eager hand,
And felt about the knee.
"'Tis clear enough the Elephant
Is very like a tree!"

The Fifth, who chanced to touch the ear,
Deny the fact who can,
"This marvel of an Elephant
Is very like a fan!"

The Sixth no sooner had begun
About the beast's tail to grope,
"I see," quoth he, "the Elephant
Is very like a rope!"

And so these men of Indostan
Disputed loud and long,
Though each was partly in the right,
And all were in the wrong!

-John Godfrey Saxe (1816-1887) (edited version)

Seek Synergy

People who think, get in sync!

Synergy is that special power that we all take for granted. We recognize it by saying: "It's the energy," "the chemistry," "the stars lined up for us," "we just clicked," "we had a meeting of minds," and "we were in the zone." It is an unexplainable experience that always leaves us saying: "WOW! That felt great!"

Synergy comes about when a project or specific job is integrated and aligned and when the team members are mentally and emotionally in sync–committed to a shared destiny.

Rather than expecting Synergy to happen by luck, chance, or fate, choose to seek Synergy by taking the initiative to look for it in every job, every function, and every relationship.

Continuous improvement is the bedfellow of Synergy. Synergy is about leaning positively into a job and seeking each day to improve quality, service, and teamwork. Make 1+1=3 by looking for ways to improve a job, connect with others and "WOW" customers. It is an optimistic, practical, and strategically prudent way to take everyday work situations and problems and focus on finding the best solutions. It's about going the extra mile with internal and external customers – exceeding their expectations. Personally, it is about doing the best job you can and then a bit extra. When people are giving a bit extra, it's not uncommon for a seemingly average team to begin achieving the extraordinary through the practice of Synergy.

Synergy always works, if you work at it. Synergy means more "we" and less "me." The key is a heightened sense of awareness. Awareness will allow you to discover the power of Synergy. When people are cooperating and combining energies in the present, there's magic in the air. Interestingly, the lowest form of energy in the universe is matter, and the highest form is mind energy. The power of directed and focused mind energy can change many things about the way you relate to yourself and the world. Great discoveries and fortunes have been made by those who have understood how to direct energy and the dynamics of related activities.

"Men stumble over the truth from time to time–but most pick themselves up and hurry off as if nothing happened."
-Winston Churchill

Like the Canadian geese, bees synergize, too. In the winter, bees create what is called the "bee winter dance." They form themselves into a ball and start moving, and the energy they create keeps the whole ball warm. The bees in the middle of the ball change and go out to the outside and the outside ones go to the inside, in a kind of shuffling dance. Through that movement, they are all able to survive the cold of winter.

The Father and His Sons

A father had a family of sons who were perpetually quarreling among themselves. When he failed to heal their disputes by his exhortations, he was determined to give them a practical illustration of the evils of disunion; and for this purpose, he one day told them to bring him a bundle of sticks. When they had done so, he placed the bundle into the hands of each of them in succession, and ordered them to break it in pieces. They tried with all their strength, and were not able to do it. He next opened the bundle, took the sticks out separately, one by one, and again put them into his sons' hands, upon which they broke them easily.

He then addressed them in these words: "My sons, if you are of one mind, and unite to assist each other, you will be as this bundle, uninjured by all the attempts of your enemies; but if you are divided among yourselves, you will be broken as easily as these sticks."

-Aesop's Fables

Talk It Out

Synergy is a conspiracy to overthrow conflict and hate!

If you're angry and upset, don't transfer your negativity on to someone else. A cat-kicker, Zig Ziglar says, is someone who kicks other people emotionally. This affects profits, productivity, and job satisfaction.

Anything can be resolved if people are willing to talk things out. Often, two people in an argument allow their egos to take over, and that's when the anger and screaming begins and resentment sets in. Work on maintaining a professional problem-solving attitude and be objective during conflict. Stay emotionally in the present and don't take things personally. Maintaining your objectivity is of immense value in resolving differences of opinion.

When Quincy Jones recently rerecorded "We Are the World" for the refugees in Haiti, he posted a huge sign outside the studio that read, "Leave your ego outside." That sign affected all the big personalities who came to take part in the recording, and synergized the performance. The song became extremely popular and came off with so much positive energy, it was felt around the world!

20 Ways to Build Trust

1. Trust begins with yourself. All relationships begin with the relationship you have with yourself.

2. Be competent in your work. You have to be trusted to do your part to make the team successful. Be predictably responsible in your actions. Make the right choices. No right thing can come from wrong thinking.

3. Be reliable. When you say you will do something, keep your word.

4. Be responsive. Respond directly to people: make eye contact, have a firm handshake, and have good manners.

5. Be accountable. Accept good and bad circumstances and situations. Don't make excuses when you fail. Be objective and fix it. Show your strength of character under adversity.

6. Be honest. Don't embellish, exaggerate, selectively leave out information, or be afraid to express your opinion. Do not lie, cheat, steal, or deceive in any way–for anyone–for any amount of money.

7. Be loyal. Self-serving people are never trusted. Loyalty has a lot to do with trusting yourself and your ability to keep the promises you make in both your personal and business relationships.

8. Transparency. Be open and share yourself to a level of acceptable comfortableness. Politely share your opinions with others. Let people know where you stand.

9. Give sincere compliments, not false flattery.

10. Authenticity. False fronts, game playing, and double standards escalate mistrust and are a barrier to good working relationships.

11. Admit your mistakes. Have the courage to admit mistakes–apologize and move on.

12. Stand up for what's right. It's not who's right that counts, it's what's the right thing to do. This is true for all of life's situations.

13. Be respectful. Being respectful to everyone demonstrates your strength of character.

14. Be fair and balanced. Be fair to all and consider how decisions will impact everyone.

15. Be open-minded. Prejudice and judgements based on your religion or cultural values will cause conflict and eliminate trust.

16. Listen. The fastest way to create resentment and resistance is to be a preoccupied bad listener.

17. Don't gossip. Remember the person who is gossiping with you, is gossiping about you.

18. Be hardworking. Everyone respects, trusts, and even admires a hardworking person who dedicates their best efforts to the job.

19. Be cooperative. Positive, cooperative people are trusted more easily.

20. Communicate consistently, avoid closed doors, and secretive agendas. Be candid and open with everyone.

SUCCESS HABIT TWO: RIGHT MENTAL ATTITUDE

Rupert and the Power of Authentic Choices

Today is Rupert's first day at work. He had slept heavily, a fitful night, tossing and turning–a night of racing thoughts and anxious images.

For as long as he can remember, his father told him: "Son, you should get a secure job with a large company that will provide you with retirement benefits and health insurance." He could still hear those words playing in his head the day he went for the interview at the bank; and when they offered him the job, he felt a sense of satisfaction knowing that his father would be proud of him. The next day, he felt conflicted and a sadness came over him at the thought of being cooped up in a cubicle all day long, dealing with numbers.

In his heart, Rupert was a nonconformist and knew that this job would require a large degree of compromise on his part. He really wanted to be a graphic artist. He loved that kind of thing–working on advertising design and animation.

When the alarm went off, he had to force himself to get out of bed. Walking across the room to the window, he drew back the drapes. It was a cloudy day and it was as if it was connected to his grey body-on-droop-mood. He could almost feel the heaviness of the clouds entering his body and weighing him down.

"I hate cloudy weather. I'm going to have a lousy day!" he thought. "I wonder if I'll be acceptable. I'll just be quiet, the same as I was at school. That always works. If you're quiet, nobody sees you."

As he fastened his belt, thoughts of school run through his mind: Flashes of his first day, elementary school, high school. "That first day was pure hell. I can still feel the pain. Everybody in a row, all standing, looking just like each other, most of all those phony teachers," he recalled. He put those thoughts out of his mind and made his way to the bank. He didn't want to be late. He arrived with a few minutes to spare and went directly to his new boss' office. She was standing in her doorway waiting for him.

"Rupert, this will be your desk; and, by the way, here at our bank, we prefer that it be kept tidy, just as you should be. Did you read the dress code regulations?"

"Yes, sir."

"Don't call me sir! My name is Ms. Ashworth."

"Yes, Ms. Ashworth."

"That's better. Now relax, Rupert. Later, you will be taken to the training school, where you will learn about the basics of our banking policies and procedures. Let me make myself clear, Rupert. If you work hard, do what you're told, be on time for work everyday, the bank is an excellent place for you to build a steady, long-term career."

"Yes, sir, I mean, Ms. Ashworth."

Rupert felt extremely uncomfortable. The environment seemed overly formal. There was very little, if any, personal interaction. He tried to make eye contact with a few people that passed his cubicle. It seemed as if everyone was hurrying around with their shoulders hunched, heads down, with expressionless eyes that looked right through you. He just sat there and waited and wondered if this was the right decision for him. Eventually, someone said, "Rupert, follow me . . ."

The day dragged on and although the information he received in training class was interesting, the monotony of the trainer's voice exhausted him. He couldn't wait to get home.

He had no sooner arrived home, when his dad asked him: "Well, how was your day, Son?"

"Dad, I don't know if this is what I want . . ."

"Now, Rupert, when I was your age, I would have been thankful for an opportunity like this. You kids of today don't appreciate anything. It was different for me

when I was your age. I would have to walk to work every day, ten miles there, ten miles back, uphill both ways."

"Yes, Dad, but I didn't do anything today; I just sat there listening to a boring guy read from a Power Point. It's as if we are just robots and they were downloading data. We were not really acknowledged as people."

"They know you are there. Everybody has their own job to do; the world doesn't revolve around you."

Rupert was an extremely aware young man and he knew that he didn't fit in. He was aware that he was surrendering what he would really like to do for this so-called secure job, mostly to please his dad. That night Rupert slept heavily, exhausted from the emotional drain of his first day.

The next morning, he had no sooner arrived at work, when he heard Ms. Ashworth bellow out his name.

"Ruuu-pert . . ."

"Yes, Ms. Ashworth?"

"Were you on time for work today?"

"Yes, Ms. Ashworth."

"You'll be in training again today. They're expecting you."

"Yes, Ms. Ashworth."

Ms. Ashworth had a reputation for being a tough boss who got the job done. "I motivate by fear," was her motto. Most people, including the bank president, avoided Ms. Ashworth. When they needed to communicate with her, it would normally be by email.

Rupert promised himself that he would never be the kind of manager, she was. "When I'm a manager one day," he thought, "I will create an environment where people will love their jobs and want to come to work and not feel as fearful as I do."

Rupert sat next to an odd-looking young man with small round, thick glasses and a plastic pen pouch sticking out of his shirt pocket. "Wow, what a nerd!" Rupert thought. But he greeted him nonetheless, and they immediately struck up a friendship. After training school that day, Rupert and his new friend, Jason, walked together to the local bus station, speculating about their future careers at the bank.

Rupert's first year went by so fast it was as if he was transported into the future in a time machine. It was full of all kinds of experiences and he began to enjoy certain parts of his job. He decided to suck up the parts he didn't enjoy and do the best job he could. At the annual conference, Rupert received his first good service award. Ms. Ashworth had now become the bank manager and Rupert her assistant. She seemed to have a glimmer of a know-it-all smile as he walked up to her to collect his award. "I told you you'd make it. Just do as you're told and one day you could be a manager, too." He cringed at the thought of doing this for the rest of his life.

Several days after the conference, Jason said, "Rupert, I'm reading this book about choosing your attitude and finding your purpose in life. Once you *find your purpose–the thing that will get you out of bed in the morning–you automatically become motivated and fulfilled. You must read it!"*

"Oh, give me a break, Jason! Motivation? What good will that do me at the bank?"

As time passed, Rupert did well, but Jason was promoted ahead of him–twice–and Rupert felt angry that he had been passed up. To top it all, he was now reporting to his friend–who he knew well–and thought he was smarter than him.

Once again he felt the same old sense of dissatisfaction. To get away from it all, Rupert thought a good vacation would help. "I'll go up to my uncle's house up north. I'll spend some time away from daily business and come back refreshed."

His uncle was different than his dad. His dad would always say that his brother Bill was unrealistic and believed in all that weird mambo jumbo motivational stuff that just cluttered up your head. Rupert always liked Uncle Bill; even though there was a serious side to his demeanor, he was approachable and relaxed.

The first day passed, pleasantries were exchanged, and laughter and stories of days gone by were shared willingly, embarrassingly, and with love.

Rupert woke up every morning well rested, feeling a sense of calmness about himself. He knew he would need to head home soon and would miss Uncle Bill and Aunt Mary. She was a quiet reserved person but when she spoke, it was always thoughtful, sensitive, and to the point.

Bill had a ritual: He would start the day off by excitedly describing it. How wonderful it was outside, how good the trees looked, and how grateful he was for just being alive. He would say crazy things like, "I choose to live this day to the fullest, because today is the only guaranteed day I have left and I need to make the most of it. I am going to have fun and make it a good one." Mary would smile, nod, and agree. At first Rupert thought this ritual was silly but it grew on him, and he began to like it and look forward to it. He liked the feeling of peace he experienced when practicing Bill's philosophy.

Bill and Mary lived in an average size dwelling sitting on a small holding of about 7 or 8 acres. Nearby, down a windy little path from the house, there was a creek from which the spring rains swelled out every year into, a small river. Rupert loved the trees that hung over the riverbank and enjoyed the crispness of the air–but more than that, he was discovering so much about life and himself. He learned that Bill was extremely smart and full of stories and observations on life. He could listen to him for hours. He realized Dad was totally wrong about his brother. Bill was pretty cool, insightful, and had a very successful life.

Bill would go down to the creek each day to fish. He would say that people said they were going fishing–but it wasn't fishing they really wanted, it was contemplation and peace. Insights like that got Rupert thinking more about what he wanted and what his purpose was. He found it easy to talk with Bill about personal things, because Bill seemed non-judgmental: he just listened, nodded, and then expanded the thought. Rupert loved that. He loved having Bill open his mind with sagely mentoring and coaching.

On one such occasion, they were sitting by the creek and Rupert said: "Bill, I don't know what my purpose is, what I'm meant to do with life."

Bill stared at Rupert for what seemed like an eternity—but Rupert didn't feel uncomfortable or uneasy. He noticed a knowing acceptance in Bill's gaze, as though he had somehow arrived at an important and meaningful turning point and Bill knew that, and knowingly acknowledged it without a word spoken.

Then, with a definiteness that Rupert had never heard in Bill's voice, he said, "Rupert, let me tell you a story that helped me change my life. This story was told to me by a great teacher, and I know he would be happy for me to pay it forward to someone ready to hear it, and I will tell it to you as I heard it.

"There was once a great builder of homes. He was renowned for his ability to build the finest quality home. He built a home for the mayor, the fire chief, and the sheriff. All the contractors in town wanted him to build houses for them.

"He would find a great sense of purpose in building a quality home. He valued great workmanship and would step back and look at his good work and feel satisfied with a job well done.

"One day he decided he did not want to work in construction any longer because although he did a great job and felt a great sense of purpose, he seldom received praise and his family didn't inquire much after his work. He decided that perhaps he should be doing a more thankful job that might get him more recognition and appreciation.

"So, he told his employer of his plans to quit. He would try something else.

"The contractor was very sorry to see him go and asked him if you could build one more house as a personal favor. He reluctantly agreed—he was the kind of man that his heart needed to be in the job and his heart was not in this job. His workmanship was only fair and even shoddy most of the time. It was sad to see a great builder lose his enthusiasm and damage his reputation this way.

"At last the contract was done and the contractor came to inspect the house. As he left, he handed the builder the front door key. 'This is your house,' he said. 'It is my gift to you!'

"The builder was shocked. He knew where he had used inferior materials. If only he knew he was building his own house, he would have put his heart into it. He would have made sure that the quality and attention to detail would have been at their highest level.

"And so, it is with us, Rupert. We build our lives a day at a time, often not putting our hearts into our work, not living out the things that we truly value, and not feeling a sense of purpose because our deeper reasons for working each day are not being satisfied. Everyday that goes by without living it to the fullest is a lost day. What are your reasons for going to work? It's not the money, Rupert, you've found that out. It's much deeper and more meaningful than that. For the builder, it was the sense of accomplishment and quality workmanship that gave him a sense of purpose. He also wanted to be recognized by those he loved but never made it known to them. Once he stopped focusing on *that, he lost his passion and his heart was not in it.*

"Find out what you value most in your life, Rupert, and then surround yourself with work that allows you to live it out each day–that's where your sense of purpose lies. When you connect to the things that drive you emotionally, it fires up your desire to excel. You will never be motivated by fear again."

Bill had just opened an entire new world to Rupert. What did he value? Was it money or was it what money could buy? "That's it! That's why I go to work, to get the money to buy security. I value the idea of being secure," he thought. "I'm afraid of failing. I'm afraid of being alone. That's why I thought I needed all that money. So, I guess what I need to do is work in an environment that offers a fair amount of security."

Rupert then realized that there were other values and needs that made him feel worthwhile, such as creativity, achievement, and recognition. He began by making a list of his values, all the things he really liked, and who he liked being around. He had just begun to own his life and that, within itself, was inspiring and life enhancing.

Rupert left Bill and Mary on a beautiful spring afternoon and as he drove through the mountains, a sense of calm and present-moment gratitude filled his every thought.

Rupert realized that he had to pursue his natural tendency toward graphic arts to enable him to live his life on purpose. With the knowledge he gained from being a banker, he prepared an outstanding business plan and secured a loan that allowed him to open his own graphic arts and design company. Under Rupert's leadership, his business grew in leaps and bounds, particularly in his natural market: the banking industry. He secured many long-term contracts and became the envy of his competitors. Rupert believes that his success came about because he found his purpose and made the authentic choices to move his life to its rightful place. He chose to have a clearly defined vision, and clearly defined performance expectations for his staff and a strong customer service culture prevails in his company–all of which are a natural extension of his authentic leadership style.

-Based on a true story.

Rupert's Credo

► Choose the right mental attitude.

► Choose awareness.

► Choose to go to work on "purpose."

► Choose to be passionate.

► Choose wisdom.

► Choose to have a vision.

► Choose winning expectations.

Choose the Right Mental Attitude

Abraham Lincoln wisely said: "Folks are just about as happy as they make their minds up to be." When I look at people in my seminars, I search for those who have made up their minds to be happy. I search for the fire in their eyes. Is there an outer reflection of an inner glowing spirit? I see many glowing, radiant, and willing—"I'm-ready-eyes" but sadly, I also see many defensive, cold, and "keep-your-distance" eyes. Almost always, "I'm-ready-eyes" contribute more, have more fun, and communicate more effectively. But then the magic happens, slowly, but surely, the "keep-your-distance-eyes" soften, become warmer, and start flickering with curiosity. And before too long, they have shifted their thinking–and once again I'm stunned by the power of positive energy. It is wild fire contagious!

Attitude describes a person's behavior based on how they choose to think and feel about people and life. Choosing the right mental attitude is accepting that every one of us is responsible for the look on our face. Right attitudes come from right thinking, which leads to clearer, quicker, and more effective communication with others. Our words travel on waves of positive or negative energy created by our attitudes, so it is important that we choose to think in ways that allow us to have a positive attitude. Body language, a certain look, a roll of the eye, and the "Elvis lip" can create huge, unspoken barriers to relationship cooperation. Negative attitudes create distancing energy barriers that result in avoidance behavior.

Some years ago, Lyall Watson, in his book *Super Nature*, demonstrated the damaging effects of negative energy on environments, including its effect on plant life. He proved with various electronic measures that plants are affected positively or negatively whenever a person enters a controlled room. If the person is hostile and angry, the plant registers erratic activity on the electronic gauges. Conversely, when cheery, laughing people entered the same room, the gauges recorded a more stable, less volatile response.

Watson's research suggests that human energy can change the environment. If this research is taken to its logical conclusion, it suggests that our energy affects the present-moment environment. Hostile, negative energy, therefore, would reflect a hostile reactionary environment. If this be true, then that's not where it ends. It means we affect and are responsible for the atmosphere, collective peace and personality of our companies, cities, and nations. It is vitally important that we accept that the right mental attitude is not only an individual responsibility, but also a collective one.

Success in life and work is about how we think and the attitudinal choices we make, and how they may lead us to foster great and rewarding relationships. Projecting the right image has become very important. How we behave influences the impression we leave with others. If we are putting on a facade (false front) even without realizing it, we are sending invisible messages of insincerity. It is far better to be an authentic reserved person with positive energy and open body language, than an artificially talkative and outgoing phony.

The right mental attitude means making authentic and empowering choices that are positive and help you grow; help others grow; and lead to actions that are healthy, honest, and honorable. Right attitudinal choices will build a foundation of strong values, self-esteem, and approachable behaviors–exactly what we need in a high-performance team.

If we make authentic choices that help us build a strong relationship with ourselves, others, and life, for the most part, we become validated, secure, and comfortable in our own skins. Secure individuals collaborate and cooperate more easily with others, and their view of life is vastly more optimistic.

Insecurity is the enemy of teamwork!

Choose Awareness

Being more conscious and in the present moment is a powerful ability, but it takes practice. Being in the present involves becoming more aware of your surroundings, others, and who you are. A consciousness of why you react and act in certain ways is a valuable life skill, especially when you feel an inner resistance to change. Knowing yourself is the path to understanding the actions and behaviors of others.

The practice of being in the present moment is the essence of problem identity and resolution. A heightened awareness also improves intuition and sensitivity to the energy around you. Therefore, it stands to reason that if your thoughts are in the past, or the future, you may not be in the present, thus making you unable to actively listen and missing details that would help you to solve a problem or make a sale.

It is so easy to let thoughts slip into the future. Living in the future is a kind of escape hatch. It helps us cope with life by pushing worry and uncertainty into a time when circumstances will hopefully be better. This is also true for living and dwelling in the past. Many people are still living with past hurts, relationships, situations, or circumstances that cannot be changed, but they still hold onto them. Such "baggage" can never be repaired by dwelling on what should have or could have been done. No one can change the past. The past is the past. It's gone and that's it. We can only rectify what's been done in the past by doing something about it now, today.

"There are the Nows, Was's and Gonna Be's. A Now is the most precious thing you can have, because a Now goes by with the speed of light. Let's say you're having a beautiful day Now, that you want to hold on to forever. No matter how much you want to hold on to it, it's going to be a Was. A lot of people get stuck in and can't let go of the Was's. Those Was's get heavy, and they start to decay into shoulda-couldas. And, they never have time for the new Now. Follow this advice and you'll be what you always felt you were Gonna Be."

-Sid Caesar, Comedian

Escapes of the Mind

Past thinkers always say:

► If only I had a different job . . .

► What I should've done is . . .

► If only I could've . . .

► I wish I could've been born rich . . .

► Sometimes, I really feel I'm stuck . . .

► We have never had the opportunity . . .

Future thinkers always say:

► When I find the right job . . .

► If I get a raise . . .

► If I get promoted . . .

► If I'm lucky . . .

► When I've got more money . . .

► When I go on holiday . . .

► When I find the right person . . .

► When my ship comes in . . .

► If the blue bird of happiness . . .

Resolutions For Today

Just for today, I will try to live through this day only, and not tackle my whole life's problem at once. I can do something for 12 hours that would appall me, if I felt I had to keep it up for a lifetime.

Just for today, I will be happy. After all, most people are about as happy as they make up their minds to be.

Just for today, I will look as agreeable as I can, dress becomingly, speak softly, act courteously, criticize not one bit and not try to improve anybody but myself.

Just for today, I will adjust myself to what is; and I will not keep trying to adjust everything else to my own desires.

Just for today, I will exercise my soul in three ways: I will do somebody a good turn, and not get found out. I will do at least two things I don't want to do, just for the exercise. And today, if my feelings are hurt, I will not show it to anyone.

Just for today, I will try to strengthen my mind. I will learn something useful. I will read something that requires effort, thought, and concentration.

Just for today, I will have a program. I may not follow it exactly, but I will have it. I will save myself from the two pests: hurry and indecision.

Just for today, I will have a quiet half-hour all by myself for meditation and relaxation. During this half-hour, I will try to get a better perspective of my life.

Just for today, I will be unafraid. Especially, I will not be afraid to enjoy what is beautiful and that, as I give to the world, so the world will give to me.

-Alcoholics Anonymous

The Six Priorities
A Do-it-Now Attitude

A management consultant was asked by a corporation president to help him improve the performance of his top 100 executives. Without a moment's hesitation the consultant said, "Put them onto a things-to-do-today-list and let them try to accomplish the six most important things that have to be done today."

Some months later, the president met with the consultant again and said to him, "You never sent me a bill for the last consultation."

"If it was of value to you, drop a check in the mail in direct proportion to its value."

Three weeks later, the consultant received a check for $10,000.

If you were doing the six most important things in your life every day, you would be accomplishing 1,440 in the moment, life changing experiences per year. Would this be a formula for success? Of course, it would!

If you don't manage change, change will manage you!

Choose to Go to Work on "Purpose"

Work can be seen as a chore or it can be seen as a deed of creation.

When we choose to do our work with honor, we demonstrate a respect for ourselves and our work becomes our contribution, our gift to the team and to the orchestra of life.

When we go to work on purpose, we shift away from being motivated by fear. We are motivated by desire. The opposite of this is when we see our work as a have to: We don't do things with the same willing attitude. Our hearts are not in it. Whenever we have to do something, rather than really wanting to, it becomes a grind. "I have to do this to pay the rent" or "I have to do this to make ends meet" leads to fear.

When we choose to go to work on purpose–and see each thing we do as a way to contribute, learn, and improve–we are motivated by desire; we want to do it. When we are motivated by desire, time stands still, energy is boundless, and we reach a state of being blissful and in sync

Results are created by our expectations!

with life and work. Being in sync can be seen as a physical glow on the skin, a twinkle in the eyes, and the radiance of a smile.

Working on purpose goes hand-in-hand with making authentic choices. The day you say, "I'm in charge of my life and I choose to make it meaningful in whatever I do," is the day you've made the most important, authentic choice of your life. It is your announcement that from this moment on you will be working and winning on purpose. After that, it's a matter of making more of the right choices, the ones that fit your purpose most closely, over and over again. Making authentic choices isn't only about choosing the right place to work–it's about how you express yourself in general.

The cliché about starving painters living in garrets makes sense because painters have to live somewhere cheap until they're established artists. Basements are usually the cheapest places, but painters can't paint in basements because they need light in order to realize their passion. So they live in attics and the tops of old warehouses. They swelter in the summer and freeze in the winter, but they gain the advantage of that great, high-up light. It's part of choosing to be a painter.

You can choose today to convert any job you are doing into a zone of inspiration that will help you grow and serve your purpose!

When you know what you want, making authentic choices comes easier than when you're not committed to a course of action.

Many people are in jobs that they fell into because they needed to work. Others have never visualized further than a paycheck, and many see work as a grind. They go to work to get what they need, to fulfill what they consider the real and important other parts of their lives.

Living our lives on purpose will mean that we get in touch with our deeper, more emotional reasons for doing things. We need to ask ourselves: "What do I value highly?" "What really motivates me?" "What will get me to live a life of enthusiasm?"

"There is joy in work. There is no happiness except in the realization that we have accomplished something."

-Henry Ford

I ask people who attend my seminars why they go to work—nobody needs to go to work. Many people get by, some way or another.

What's the real reason?

"Money," everyone says.

What are you going to do with all that money?

"Educate my kids; buy a home; go back to college."

The real motivator is always what the money can do, what it can bring. Money is a means to an end but never the end within itself. Where are the programs in our schools to teach subjects such as achieving a sense of purpose or building self-esteem? Wouldn't it be amazing if we had a subject on building character and achieving goals in life?

It's never too late to find your purpose and find the reason that will ignite you with passion, and if brought to work, will be noticed and rewarded in two very distinct ways: Greater job security and deeper job satisfaction.

"He who has a 'why' to live for, can bear almost any 'how'."

-Nietzsche

Choose to be Passionate

Come to work on purpose and your passion will come to work with you. Obviously, no one's going to be delighted with every aspect of their work all the time, but it's vital to have a central core of enjoyment or pleasure so that when things get tough, you still have the emotional security to get through it. If you ever watch the Food Network, you'll see people who are in love with their jobs. The chefs talk about the food, compare flavors and colors, taste and smell things, and have a great time doing it. But the next time you go to a restaurant, look at the chaos, the heat and flames in the kitchen, the demanding physical aspects of the work. To be a chef, to work all day and half the night on your feet in a hot kitchen with people yelling, dishes clattering, and hungry, cranky customers, well–you'd better love food!

When you love your work, it's easy to commit to being great at it, to seek out improvements in yourself, and to challenge yourself by taking on new tasks or learning new skills. When you are committed in this way, you are modeling passion and commitment to your team. It also directly impacts the most important people in any business–the customers. Exceptional customer service means more than making the customer happy today: It means making each customer a customer for life! Being willing to go the extra mile with your customers will keep bringing them back. Bringing passion to work will flow over into better service, product quality, continuous improvement, teamwork, and communications. Passion energizes the workplace with enthusiasm, and we all know that enthusiasm sells! Passion is contagious and inspiring and is one of the keys to making any business soar.

"The human race has one effective weapon . . . and that's laughter."

-Mark Twain

Choose Wisdom

An individual who has experienced life and approaches it with balanced, clear thinking; knowledge of humanity and nature; the ability to enthusiastically communicate and direct energy and creativity toward a worthy vision and goal, would be considered wise by many.

Choosing wisdom means choosing to work with all our areas of intelligence: emotional, social, academic, creative, logical, physical, personal, and spiritual.

Sadly, of course, our society is still into the outdated concept that academic ability equals wisdom. It is my experience that different situations in life require different approaches. An academically intelligent person has the ability to learn and retain information, but may not have any social intelligence. I believe, that every individual has their own special intelligence. It is the discovery, acceptance, and development of this intelligence that builds unique wisdom. There are also many individuals who have manifested more than one intelligence.

Emotional Intelligence is coming to terms with our emotions, both positive and negative. It is being in touch with our feelings and having the ability to understand how others feel.

Social Intelligence is the ability to communicate ideas, to interact with others, and understand the needs of individuals and communities.

Academic Intelligence is the ability to analyze, assimilate, and learn facts, strategies, skills, and formulas, and maintain a level of knowledge for later use–as in a preferred profession or occupation.

Creative Intelligence is the ability to create and build something within the framework of one's own mind. To creatively express ideas, music, art forms, business formulas, paintings, songs, sculpting, computer programs, and so on.

Logical Intelligence is the ability to think clearly with emotional detachment–to clearly calculate step-by-step processes and plans.

Physical Intelligence is being in touch with our bodies and understanding why our bodies react in certain ways. It's knowing and loving the house we occupy.

Personal Intelligence is clearly knowing what's good and bad and changing what needs to be changed. It's about making authentic choices, having a purpose, and fulfilling our dreams.

Spiritual Intelligence is the greatest intelligence of all, because it means we are not insecure about what we have or don't have. When we have spiritual intelligence, we know that we are a part of something great and wonderful. We are living our lives serving, contributing, and growing with grace. Our disposition is one of gratefulness and yet, our inner strength is very real and visible.

"What the mind can conceive and believe, the mind will achieve."

-Napoleon Hill

Choose to Have a Vision

Imagination is the playground of potential.

The power of visualizing success and the power of imagination to achieve a sense of fulfillment are unique human qualities. Visualizing offers us an incredible opportunity to learn new and exciting skills, as well as make changes in our way of thinking. When we visualize ourselves performing in a particular way, it is virtually the same as if we are actually physically doing it.

Visualization has a marked effect on our health and can even help us improve our golf games, sales presentations and many other aspects of our lives.

The ability to consciously dream is a creative phenomenon, which usually begins by seeing in our minds the end result of what we desire. Desire, coupled with visualization can imprint the subconscious mind with images of success. If repeated consciously, consistently, and daily with enough emotion, the mind accepts these images as fact, translates them into reality through the mind-body connection and thus, the physical reality becomes apparent.

Choose Winning Expectations

"If we were to begin, even in grade school, to teach everyone the simple lessons of human relations–just as we teach reading, writing, and arithmetic–it would have a profound effect on the world we live in. This task represents perhaps the greatest challenge which education faces today and in centuries to come."

-Dr. William J. Riley

An amazing discovery by researchers of quantum physics is that the results of research can be affected by the expectation of the researcher, because the researcher introduces a personal energized vision into the existing energy field. The combination of the two changes the outcome. We know this to be true from person to person. For example, when a teacher has a high expectation of performance from a child, the child normally lives up to that expectation. Yet, for some reason, in business, this truth has not been followed through to its logical conclusion. If we followed this quantum physics paradigm, we could find ways of raising expectations positively and influence many environments that need it.

The business world thrives on high energy, ideas, and innovations. They are the life blood of existence. New products, solutions, and concepts create new markets and growth. The principles of continuous improvement are now the cornerstone of many successful American businesses.

Where does this power source originate? It originates from the single individual within a team who has the passion, purpose, and expectation to win. We all have choices and we can choose to focus our talents, gifts, and abilities toward a worthy goal, powerfully increasing our potential for success. We can create happiness and joy. To create happiness, we can choose to have dinner with good friends and find ourselves laughing and having a good time. Happiness is an external event. We can create joy by living our lives passionately, on purpose, and being grateful for the abundance that surrounds us. Joy is an inside job. Why not expect to be happy? Why not expect to create extraordinary joy in your life?

Choosing to have a winning expectation for yourself and your team will make all the difference in your performance. Expect to solve your problems. Expect to succeed as a team. Expect to succeed in all relationships. Success is an inside job. It is having the mind-set and focus on creating something greater than the obvious–focusing on achieving more than what you can see. Some people say: "When I see it, I will believe it." They should say: "When I believe it, I will see it."

The aphorism, 'As a man thinketh in his heart so is he,' not only embraces the whole of a man's being, but is so comprehensive as to reach out to every condition and circumstance of his life. A man is literally what he thinks, his character being the complete sum of all his thoughts.

As the plant springs from, and could not be without, the seed, so every act of a man springs from the hidden seeds of thought, and could not have appeared without them. This applies equally to those acts called 'spontaneous' and 'unpremeditated' as to those which are deliberately executed.

Act is the blossom of thought, and joy and suffering are its fruits; thus does a man garner in the sweet and bitter fruitage of his own husbandry.

> *"Thought in the mind hath made us, what we are*
>
> *By thought was wrought and built. If a man's mind*
>
> *Hath evil thoughts, pain comes on him as comes*
>
> *The wheel the ox behind . . . If one endures*
>
> *In purity of thought, joy follows him*
>
> *As his own shadow - sure."*
>
> *-James Allen*
> *"As a Man Thinketh"*

"The longer I live, the more I realize the impact of attitude on life. Attitude, to me, is more important than facts. It is more important:

- ► *than the past,*

- ► *than education,*

- ► *than money,*

- ► *than circumstances,*

- ► *than failures,*

- ► *than successes, than what other people think, say or do.*

It can make or break a company, a church, or a home. The remarkable thing is that everyday we have a choice regarding the attitude we will embrace for that day.

We cannot change our past . . .

We cannot change the fact that people will act in a certain way.

We cannot change the inevitable.

The only thing we can do is play on the one string we have, and that is our attitude. I am convinced that life consists of 10% of what happens to me and 90% on how I react to it. And, so it is . . . we are in charge of our attitudes."

-Charles Swindoll
"Attitude"

Jack's Letter

Hi Chris,

Driving home I was thinking about your presentation. I understood your message but my immediate thoughts were: "He should have my job for a day." I am a glass-is-half-full kind of person and it did occur to me that I had never made a deliberate choice to have a great day – every day, so I decided to follow your instructions.

The next morning I got out of bed, slapped my hands together and said, "Today, I'm gonna have a great day." I felt absolutely foolish doing that! While I was shaving I told myself, "This day belongs to me, nobody's going to take it away from me; not the truck on the freeway or the problems I would face, or the people in the office. This is my day."

So, for the next three weeks, I practiced this daily ritual, which extended into the office; when I came in, I would greet everyone in a relaxed, cheerful manner. I would say to the receptionist: "Good morning, how are you today?!"

She'd smile and respond with, "I am fine and how are you, Jack?"

I would respond enthusiastically: "I'm having a great day today."

When I met people in the hallway, they would say, "Hi, Jack, how are you?"

And, again I would respond enthusiastically and say, "I'm having a great day today."

Then . . . I had one of those lousy days. There was that truck on the freeway, – everything that could go wrong - did. I blustered through the office door and my receptionist said, "Hi, Jack, how are you?"

I just ignored her. I didn't have time for this Synergy nonsense.

I walked into the first meeting, to a cheery greeting, "Hi, Jack, how are you?" people asked.

To my surprise out slipped: "I'm having a great day, thank you."

Throughout the day, as people greeted me, before I could stop myself, I replied: "I'm having a great day."

The more I said it, the more my mood lifted!

Chris, by the end of the day, my mood changed all together. I realized I had conditioned myself to be more positive, and this Synergy "nonsense" was powerful stuff. I notice that I'm more relaxed, I don't have as many headaches and I have less stress-related back pain.

Thank you for all the good work you do and this helpful technique, it really works!

Have a great day and I'll see you at our next Synergy workshop,

Jack

Talent wins games, but teamwork and intelligence wins championships

-Michael Jordan

20 Ways to Have the Right Mental Attitude

1. Exercise your privilege of choice and always look at the bright side of life.

2. Have an attitude of gratitude. Be grateful for your ability to work, for your health, family, friendship, and life.

3. Take "me-time" once a day. Listen to your favorite music–talk with a good friend–read something worthwhile–take a walk.

4. Ramp up your curiosity–learn how other jobs connect to yours.

5. Learn something new every day–new computer skills, selling, marketing, business writing, P.R., leadership and management skills.

6. Practice continuous improvement, make 1+1=3. Be aware and notice more things about your job and workplace, and make suggestions for improvement.

7. Quit complaining.

8. Turn a weakness into a strength.

9. Be passionate–get involved.

10. Give people hugs.

11. Be a participator–don't stand on the sidelines.

12. Have pride in what you do–do everything as well as you can!

13. Recognize your personal strengths and talents and how they contribute to the success of your team.

14. Take initiative and be a workplace leader–don't stand back–Synergy is about involvement and helping.

15. Choose a job you love–or choose to love the personal growth you gain from what you're doing. All work is honorable.

16. Motivate and encourage others.

17. Deal with conflict right away.

18. Stop gossip and stay away from gossip.

19. Don't say "yes" when you want to say "no."

20. Choose to create joy in your life by improving the relationship with yourself, others, and life.

SUCCESS HABIT THREE: MAKE IT FUN!

Fun Is Serious Business

"Here we go again; I wonder what it is this time." thought Maryann. She had just been summoned once more to June's office. June was her new boss and Divisional President and had a dislike for all things H.R. She would refer to it as the touchy-feely department.

Maryann took a deep breath, straightened up, and confidently walked into June's office, "You wanted to see me."

"You bet! It's about your agenda for the quarterly meeting. What the heck is this about a game? I don't agree with it!"

"What's the problem?"

"Well," June said sarcastically, "I don't know if you have noticed, but business sucks and you want to play a game. What's that all about?"

Maryann detested June's leadership style and realized instantly that this was going to be another one of June's you-will-change-it-modify-it-until-I-like-it-confrontational meetings. What a bitch!

Unlike all the other times, Maryann thought, "I'm ready to take her on! She won't bully me this time! I'm going to take a stand–this is right! And I'm not going to change the agenda! Screw her!"

Maryann and June are total opposites! Maryann is a quiet, soft spoken person, but she has a fire in her eyes and a slight contented smile that always seems to be there. Her steady consistent confident demeanor makes her approachable and well-liked.

June is a small, wiry, talkative, feisty woman who is extremely bright; but when it comes to social intelligence, she's a Neanderthal! She lacks empathy and understanding on a level rarely seen in today's world. You could say, June is anti-fun. She believes people are paid to work, not play games and make fools of themselves.

Maryann looked June directly in the eye "June, there is a reason we make meetings fun. There's always a message and the staff retains more of it and they love it."

"Business is serious, Maryann."

"Well, so is a game of chess, but people have fun doing it, June" she said firmly.

"Well, what I want to do is get in, get the message over, and get out. I have a lot to do and my time is money!" She felt a flash of anger that she was justifying herself to Maryann. She quickly calmed herself because she had been warned numerous times about her temper by the Board of Directors. They insisted that she improve her social skills and self-awareness because of her bad reputation for rubbing people the wrong way.

Maryann saw the change in June's attitude. She was calmer. So, she jumped in quickly and took advantage of the opening that June had given her. "June, besides the game, there is something you can do to help the meeting. Would you set the tone for the day? This is an opportunity for you to connect with the staff."

"What do you mean 'set the tone'?"

"Well, June, first, I would like you to be relaxed and casual, do not prepare a speech or dress in a business suit."

"I can understand that being more casual could relax everyone, but I'm still not sold on the game idea; why would you want to play a game?"

"June, people produce more when they're having fun at work. There is less absenteeism, firings, and lawsuits when people enjoy their work . . . and they don't shoot each other! It makes them feel that their jobs are worthwhile and there is credible research to back it up."

This was the first time Maryann saw June in silent contemplation. Was she actually thinking about it? Wa-hoo!

"What are the messages, Maryann?"

"The main message is working together and supporting the company's vision and goals. You will definitely enjoy the game. I would appreciate it if you would join in."

"I don't really think . . . well okay. It won't be easy, but I suppose I should show the Board of Directors and the staff my human side."

"Thank you, June. Your involvement will contribute a lot to the meeting."

Maryann left June's office feeling elated. "WOW, that was great! Not only did she back down, but it felt like I had a personal breakthrough with her. This was a victory for fun! Maybe she's not such a bitch after all!"

If It's Not Fun, It's Not Worth It

When people come to work because they are having fun and enjoy the people they work with, the organizational culture abounds with positive energy. It becomes a place without fear – a place of play and creativity, growing and developing, and oozing with every increasing potential. It grows richer, stronger and more collaborative because of the willingness to work together.

Researchers who have worked with concepts like joy in the workplace and making work fun have found that people who enjoy their work are healthier, recover quicker from illness and injury, work more productively, are more creative, and have greater self-esteem and emotional balance. People who are happy at work don't need to take "mental health" days from their sick leave. They don't sabotage equipment or shirk their duties, and they don't shoot one another. Making work fun helps organizations succeed by helping people engage, which manifests into employee satisfaction resulting in billions of dollars gained. The question is, when it comes to your organization, are they billions gained or billions lost?

I have a colleague who once worked for the sales department of the Vermont Teddy Bear

Company in Shelburne, Vermont. At Christmas time, this company really shifts into high gear and people rotate positions as necessary. One day, word came up from the factory floor that there was a great need to get the teddy bears ready for shipping. Several people went down to the factory where they brushed and dressed and boxed teddy bears for several hours, working as a team, helping each other get each bear presentable and ready to ship. They played upbeat music and lugged heavy boxes from one part of the floor to another. They had a ball! Years later, my colleague still talks about her time at Vermont as one of her most enjoyable work experiences. The fun of doing something new as a team made work fun, and having fun made the work more easily achievable.

I'm not nearly as worried about the unemployment crisis as I am the employment crisis. If everyone who's unhappy at work decided not to go in tomorrow, the country would come to a grinding halt. It's a critical problem that so many people are so unhappy at work. There are a number of simple solutions to the lack of motivation responsibility and accountability we see in today's workplace. With the right kind of attention, and a return to ethical ideas like honesty, leadership, and open communication, we can change the workplace to being beneficial to shareholders, staff, and customers. I have seen it happen in large corporations, medium and small companies, and non-profits. They have all embraced the power of fun and became breeding grounds for teamwork, productivity, and employee satisfaction.

At Southwest Airlines, for example, fun, respect, and communication excellence are of paramount importance in creating a sense of meaning and joy in the workplace. In my opinion, one of the keys to Southwest's success is understanding that people want to work in an environment that is enjoyable, and customers like to deal with a company that enjoys what they are doing and exudes enthusiasm.

The majority of people within Southwest– including the leadership (starting with Herb Kelleher, Chairman of the Board; James Parker, CEO; and Colleen Barrett, President and COO) –believe that Southwest Airlines was created for and by its people.

Words like fun, celebration, compassion, and innovation shore up the company values, which are held in high esteem. As the most profitable airline in the U.S., Southwest not only maintains a spirit of "fun" but also has the ability to "synergize" a number of essential operational areas; thus, its well-orchestrated strategic coordination has created a competitive advantage that is difficult to match, a testimony to that old adage: When teamwork, quality, and service go up, costs come down.

Having Fun with Customers

L aughing and having a fun experience with customers is an important part of Southwest's culture and as such, humor is encouraged at every level of the organization. People are hired for their attitudes and then trained for skills. Flight attendants are encouraged to make the "in-flight safety lecture" and their other announcements more fun and entertaining. Here are some real examples that have been reported:

"There may be fifty ways to leave your lover, but there are only four ways out of this airplane "

"We do feature a smoking section on this flight; if you must smoke, contact a member of the flight crew and we will escort you out onto the wing of the airplane."

"Smoking in the lavatories is prohibited. Any person caught smoking in the lavatories will be asked to leave the plane.

"Should the cabin lose pressure, oxygen masks will drop from the overhead area. Please place the bag over your own mouth and nose before assisting children or adults acting like children."

"As you exit the plane, please make sure to gather all of your belongings. Anything left behind will be distributed evenly among the flight attendants. Please do not leave unwanted children or spouses."

"Last one off the plane must clean it."

"That was quite a bump and I know what ya'll are thinking. I'm here to tell you it wasn't the airline's fault, it wasn't the pilot's fault, it wasn't the flight attendants' fault–it was the asphalt!!"

"Welcome aboard Southwest . . . to operate your seat belt, insert the metal tab into the buckle, and pull tight. It works just like every other seat belt, and if you don't know how to operate one, you probably shouldn't be out in public unsupervised. In the event of a sudden loss of cabin pressure, oxygen masks will drop from the ceiling. Stop screaming, grab the mask, and pull it over your face. If you have a small child traveling with you, secure your mask before assisting with theirs. If you are traveling with two small children, decide now which one you love more."

"Weather at our destination is fifty degrees with some broken clouds, but they'll try to have them fixed before we arrive. Thank you, and remember, nobody loves you, or your money, more than Southwest Airlines."

An award should go to the United Airlines gate agent in Denver for being smart and funny and making her point, when confronted with a passenger who probably deserved to fly as cargo.

A flight was canceled. A single agent was re-booking a long line of inconvenienced travelers. Suddenly, an angry passenger pushed his way to the desk. He slapped his ticket down on the counter and said, "I have to be on this flight and it has to be first class."

The agent replied, "I'm sorry, sir. I'll be happy to try to help you, but I've got to help these folks first, and I'm sure we'll be able to work something out."

The passenger was unimpressed. He asked loudly, so that everyone behind him could hear, "Do you have any idea who I am?"

Without hesitating, the gate agent smiled, grabbed her public address microphone, and said, "May I have your attention, please?" she began, her voice bellowing throughout the terminal. "I have a passenger here at the gate who doesn't know who he is. If anyone in the airport can help him find out who he is, please come to gate 17." Everyone laughed, including the angry passenger. Humor won the day!

"Angels fly because they take themselves lightly."

-Jean Cousteau

What Stuffy People Think About Fun at Work

► Having fun at work is not professional.

► Having fun means we have to go off-site, which costs money.

► Laughter at work equals irresponsibility and not taking work seriously.

► Having fun should be allowed from time to time.

► Having fun will compromise results.

► Employees are paid to do a job, not have fun.

► Okay! The fun is over. Now go back to work.

"Never doubt that a group of thoughtful committed citizens can change the world, indeed it's the only thing that ever does."

-Our Values, The Body Shop

"If It's Not Fun, Why Do It?"

That's one of the phrases you will hear at Ben & Jerry's. According to Ben Cohen and Jerry Greenfield, "Everything we do in our business is value-led" and it's true that their success has been based, in large part, on their connection with human values.

From the very beginning, one of their sayings was: "How can we serve you better?" It wasn't just a customer service training line, it was for real and they meant it. That sincerity and steadfastness has earned a kind of customer loyalty that most corporations pay millions to achieve. Ben & Jerry's works from the principle advocated in this book, they focus on Synergy–seeking out ways to serve so that the sum was always greater than the separate parts.

In 1978, Ben & Jerry's started out with three goals:

1. To have fun;

2. Make a living; and

3. Give back to the community.

Customers love cheerful people and want to be around them.

As the company grew, they connected with many others who felt the same, and their ideals become a reality. In Ben & Jerry's words: "Value-led business is based on the idea that business has a responsibility to the people and the society that make its existence possible. In order to do that, values must be led and be right up there in a company's mission statement, strategy, and operating plan. This gives the employees and customers a relationship that is based on more than money. It's okay to have fun, and it's okay to be joyful."

Ben & Jerry's created what they call "The Joy Gang" with this mission: Their goal,"To keep work from being a grind." The Joy Gang plans fun events ranging from bimonthly massages for workers to an Elvis-Presley-Day, that includes an Elvis impersonator and look-alike competition, the whole idea being to bring joy into the workplace. To top that, the company has an outstanding benefits package! Now that's caring capitalism at its best!

Recently, Ben & Jerry's was sold to Unilever, and it will be a great day for business if their social mission slowly influences this worldwide conglomerate.

Research has shown us that:

▶ A child smiles at least 400 times a day.

▶ A 35-year-old only smiles 10 times a day.

▶ Most adults think they smile one-third more than they do.

▶ Laughter benefits healing and recovery from illness.

▶ Laughter releases endorphins that makes us feel good.

▶ Laughter boosts our immune system.

▶ Laughter burns up to 5 calories every minute.

▶ Laughter defuses anger.

▶ Humor and laughter create an environment of enjoyment.

▶ Laughter is the great communication connector.

▶ All the world loves a cheerful person and wants to be around them."

*I couldn't ask for a better company . . .
when you have been treated so well,
it's hard not to appreciate it. And I'm
not the only one – that's the best part
of it. They do it for everyone."*

-Julie Labor, Production Line Worker at Ben & Jerry's

Fun Elevates Healthy Emotions

A good team player makes work fun, using humor to defuse anger and disagreement. Humor in the workplace builds personal relationships and creates a climate of acceptance. It creates healthy, secure work environments. When you laugh, you program your immune system with health. Laughter pops the stress corks. It gets rid of conflict and those tense awkward moments that can exist in a busy workplace.

So, when you're under stress, look for something humorous to do, look for something funny to say, and enjoy yourself. Laughter is more contagious than tears.

He who laughs last,
doesn't get the joke!

Laughter Is the Great Connector

Laughter is a fruit of life, and it's sweetness brings joy and connection to all within its sound. A good belly laugh is physiologically and emotionally healthy. Have you noticed that nobody wants to laugh out loud anymore? Do you realize that we now have comedy clubs where we go to have a few drinks to loosen up and laugh. It's sad indeed to see individuals taking themselves too seriously. I want to remind them that connection and laughter are the great healers. If someone has a hearty belly laugh, most people will pretend they don't hear it, and some may even frown upon it; but if the laughter continues, something amazing happens. The air fills up with positive energy, the atmosphere warms up, and the laughter becomes contagious. Human beings have physiological and instinctive ways of releasing pressure and stress. Laughter, crying, sneezing, and other natural releases assist the body to feel good. Of all these, however, laughter has the greatest physical and mental therapeutic value.

In his book *The Anatomy of an Illness*, Norman Cousins describes the value of laughter in dealing with Ankylosing Spondylitis this way.

"Even before we had completed arrangements for moving out of the hospital we began the part of the program calling for the full exercise of the affirmative emotions as a factor in enhancing body chemistry. It was easy enough to hope and love and have faith, but what about laughter? Nothing is less funny than being flat on your back with all the bones in your spine and joints hurting. A systematic program was indicated. A good place to begin, I thought, was with amusing movies. Allen Funt, producer of the television program 'Candid Camera,' sent films of some of his Candid Camera classics, along with a motion picture projector. The nurse was instructed in its use. We were even able to get our hands on some old Marx Brothers films. We pulled down the blinds and turned on the machine.

It worked. I made the joyous discovery that ten minutes of genuine belly laughter had an anesthetic effect and would give me at least two hours of pain-free sleep. When the pain-killing effect of the laughter wore off, we would switch on the motion picture projector again, and, not infrequently, it would lead to another pain-free sleep interval. Sometimes the nurse read to me out of a trove of humor books. Especially useful were E.B. and Katharine White's 'Subtreasury of American Humor' and Max Eastman's 'The Enjoyment of Laughter.' How scientific was it to believe that laughter–as well as the positive emotions in general–was affecting my body chemistry for the better? If laughter did in fact have a salutary effect on the body's chemistry, it seemed at least theoretically likely that it would enhance the system's ability to fight the inflammation. So we took sedimentation rate readings just before as well as several hours after the laughter episodes. Each time there was a drop of at least five points. The drop in itself was not substantial, but it held and was cumulative. I was greatly elated by the discovery that there is a physiological basis for the ancient theory that laughter is good medicine."

Enough said, if this doesn't convince you to be happier, put the book down.

Laughter is a spiritual eruption!

Joy in the Workplace Is a Powerful Motivator

A feeling of joy is reaching a point where all our thoughts, feelings, and actions are in complete harmony with our purpose. It is being and feeling in sync with the Universe. It is a state of complete bliss. Joy is being comfortable with where you are and your role in the incredible Synergy taking place within and around you.

Joy is the euphoric feeling that is experienced when a plan comes together. It is when intense goal setting and energy have been expended and the expected result has been achieved. It is that feeling of arrival and contentment. It is the feeling of love and peace with the world. Joy is the reward of living life on purpose. Purposeful living always manifests in joy.

We can have all the wealth and power in the world and, most likely, the friends that gather around will be those who want the things we have. Material things are very fleeting. Everything can disappear in a flash.

Pleasure from material things is short-lived but joy is long lasting. Joy is a spiritual awakening and a deep knowing that all is well. When we have inner joy, we are at peace with ourselves. We love life, others, and ourselves.

Enthusiasm Is Contagious

Enthusiasm can be described as the outer reflection of an inner burning glow. I have never thought that anybody should have any other attitude toward life than enthusiasm. In every endeavor in life, personal enthusiasm is indispensable. Enthusiasm makes an average singer a superstar, an average golfer a champion. Whenever we meet people who radiate enthusiasm, we are naturally attracted to their energy. They have a glow, a positive aura–and it's contagious.

As I write this, I think of my dog Rusty. He, like all dogs, was blessed with natural enthusiasm. It was a pleasure to see how excited he got when he saw me get out of my car. He would bring a smile to my face. He would say hello by wagging his entire body. Animals know how to welcome you home.

Enthusiasm is linked to an optimistic view of life, situation or outcome and is reflected in one's personality. The best example of enthusiasm and excitement for life is found in young children. They are always excited and motivated to begin each day with gusto. It is never to late to have a happy childhood. We need to be more childlike and let our natural instincts shine. We need to bring out our love for life and let go of all the pretentiousness that distracts us from who we really are.

That's Grandpa!

One day a salesman was on a country business road trip and was caught in a storm. Dangerous lightning and the heavy rain forced him to look for shelter. Close to the road he saw a farmhouse, and made his way over to it. Drenched he knocks on the door and to his surprise a beautiful young woman opens the door and invites him in to take shelter. He thinks to himself, "This is my lucky day! – finding shelter from the storm and in the company of this charming young woman."

As they look out the window at the flowing river, he sees a hat floating on top of the water. Just then the hat begins to move across the water, going to one end of the yard and then returning to the other.

Startled and amazed, the salesman inquires, "What's that?"

"Oh, don't worry, that's only Grandpa."

"What do you mean that's Grandpa?"

"Grandpa is a very enthusiastic and determined man. He said, "Come heck or high water, I'm going to mow the lawn today!"

Excitement Is the Fiery Ember of Desire

Excitement is a feeling induced by a desire to live life to the fullest. Feeling excited is directly connected to seeing the potential of achieving a worthy goal or experiencing a highly held value-the anticipation of great things to come. This is success in its embryonic form. Excitement is one of the embers of the motivation emotion–desire. There are no great ideas, just excited people who desire to make them great. A desire to achieve success is essential for a fulfilled life.

Excitement, like enthusiasm, creates a charismatic glow in an individual. It is a "glowing" (i.e., she's just glowing with love and excitement about her future with him.) This glow is seen in anyone who is totally and passionately absorbed and caught up in the belief that life is about living. The glow is the positive energy we feel when we meet that special someone for the first time. The glow is energy personified, which engulfs and surrounds us. The glow is an influencing factor and can be seen in many leaders who have a passion and purpose for life.

This same glow can be seen in students and delegates in my seminar rooms. When I see it, I warm to it, and it excites me and energizes my presentations. It's a sign of the spirit rising up. The glow is something that can and must be turned on and left on permanently. All great business deals, all great works of art, all creative innovative work begins with the glow of excitement.

"God serves man, but is not a servant."

-Life Is Beautiful

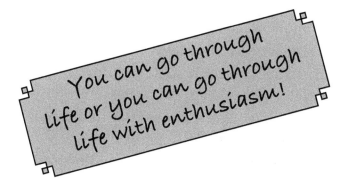

You can go through life or you can go through life with enthusiasm!

Gratitude Unlocks the Door to a Fuller Life

An attitude of gratitude speaks more about the character of the person than the act itself. Gratitude is a positive, uplifting, and thankful view of life. It says we are happy to be here and that we are grateful for life's smallest blessings.

All to often, we are unable to feel gratitude, because we live in a world where gratitude and thankfulness are seen as weaker, softer elements not to be displayed. It is sad times we live in when we cannot realize how good we have it.

By comparison, the average American family has the best standard of living in the world. The majority of people have one or even two cars per household, wall-to-wall carpeting, chairs, tables and appliances, the latest computer game, the Internet and, for the big kids, burgers for a couple of dollars and super-sized waistlines for an extra dime. We have the fastest service in the world for just about everything. Microwaveable meals in three minutes and by the time you finish reading this, it will be down to a minute.

The faster we get what we want, the more impatient we become. We want things instantly, *now*! We have developed an attitude of instant gratification. Quick fixes for everything. Quick food, quick haircuts, quick books to read, quick workouts, quick oil changes, quick relationships -the list goes on and on. Sadly, our impatience has led to an imbalance in our expectations of daily life. Expectations based on impatience have led to an attitude of irritation and frustration and, in turn, a lack of gratitude for what we have and respect for the needs of other people and society as a whole.

The solution is not in the speed of life, but in the quality of life. Relationships, and life as a whole, have unfortunately been affected by growing self-centeredness: an I-want-it-now entitlement attitude.

An attitude of gratitude is the essence of joy because it opens up our hearts and allows us to feel validated and satisfied with life. It keeps us humble and centered, and eliminates envy and greed. It helps us recognize how important it is to appreciate life in spite of the circumstances of the moment. Gratitude helps us laugh and be merry. Gratitude is about appreciating who we love and who loves us. Gratitude is not being subservient, but serving.

Gratitude is living in the realm of contribution and service, and creating a loving environment. Gratitude and fun are indispensable to living an enriching life.

The $1,000 Lemon

A local club was so sure that one of its members was the strongest man around, they offered a standing $1,000 bet.

The member would squeeze a lemon until all the juice ran into a glass and then hand the lemon to a patron. Anyone who could squeeze one more drop of juice out would win the money.

Many people had tried over time (weight lifters, longshoremen, etc.), but nobody could do it.

One day a scrawny little man came in, wearing thick glasses and a polyester suit, and said in a tiny, squeaky voice, "I'd like to try the bet."

After the laughter had died down, a club member took a lemon and squeezed all the juice out and then handed the wrinkled remains of the rind to the little man.

The crowd's laughter turned to total silence as the little man clenched his fist around the lemon and six more drops fell into the glass.

As the crowd cheered, the club member paid the $1,000 and asked the little man, "What do you do for a living? Are you a lumberjack, a weight-lifter, or what?"

The man replied sheepishly, "I work for the IRS."

Grandma Goes to Court

In a trial, a Southern small-town prosecuting attorney called his first witness, a grandmotherly, elderly woman to the stand. He approached her and asked, "Mrs. Jones, do you know me?"

She responded, "Why, yes, I do know you, Mr. Williams. I've known you since you were a boy, and frankly, you've been a big disappointment to me. You lie, you cheat on your wife, and you manipulate people and talk about them behind their backs. You think you're a big shot when you haven't the brains to realize you'll never amount to anything more than a two-bit paper pusher. Yes, I know you."

The lawyer was stunned. Not knowing what else to do, he pointed across the room and asked, "Mrs. Jones, do you know the defense attorney?"

She again replied, "Why, yes, I do. I've known Mr. Bradley since he was a youngster, too. He's lazy, bigoted, and he has a drinking problem. He can't build a normal relationship with anyone, and his law practice is one of the worst in the entire state. Not to mention he cheated on his wife with three different women. One of them was your wife. Yes, I know him."

The defense attorney nearly died. The judge asked both counselors to approach the bench and, in a very quiet voice said, "If either of you idiots asks her if she knows me, I'll send you both to the electric chair!"

-Author Unknown

Become a Synergy Funologist

Become a funologist and you will reduce your stress, become more popular and feel great every day. Funologists make relationships work by connecting in positive, humorous ways that put others at ease. Funologists choose to deliberately experience enjoyment in life. Funology can manifest itself in things like outfits, songs, recipes, work, movies and getting to know new people. To funologists, fun is never silly, it is the opposite of silly, it is the essence of a happy life, enjoyable job, and it frees them up to be vulnerable and to feel relationally enriched. It reduces the anxiety associated with fitting in. Fun is a great equalizer. It makes people instinctively care for one another and it's uniquely human.

Words for True "Funologists":

► Sunrise	Fun-rise
► Sunset	Fun-set
► Sunbeam	Fun-beam
► Sunshine	Fun-shine
► Sunday	Fun-day
► Sunbaked	Fun-baked
► Sundown	Fun-down
► Sun glow	Fun-glow
► Sun lover	Fun lover
► Fantastic	Fun-tastic
► Functional	Fun-tional
► Fundamental	Fun-duh-mental
► Phenomenon	Fun-nomenon
► Fanatics	Fun-atics
► Sunbath	Fun-bath
► Sundial	Fun-dial
► Sunflower	Fun-flower
► Sun god	Fun-god

20 Ways to Make it Fun

1. Make the choice that fun is good for you, your business, and your team.

2. Make work and play a fun-damental part of team communications.

3. Communicate with humor–it's the great connector.

4. Choose a positive attitude and look on the bright side of life.

5. Give sincere compliments and applaud the strengths of others.

6. Eliminate gossip, destructive competition, back-stabbing, and politics.

7. Get to know your teammates. Circulate a list of 10 likes and dislikes of everyone.

8. Have a personal sharing day. Share family photos by email, Facebook, or personally.

9. Schedule team get-togethers: Spring break, summer concerts, BBQ's, sports events, etc.

10. Have a dress-up competition: Christmas, Halloween, St. Patrick's Day, etc.

11. Get your team involved in a nonprofit, build a house, paint a dormitory.

12. Make fitness and health fun. Work together to improve health and fitness.

13. Plan cross-cultural theme lunches (e.g., Mexican, Hawaiian, Chinese, etc.).

14. Set up a movie night in the summer at someone's home.

15. Have the Golden Rule Day: Everyone dresses up and is on their best behavior, being Ladies and Gentlemen, saying "please" and "thank you."

16. Best recipe competition: Have individuals bring in their best recipe and award prizes.

17. Company Idol: Encourage musicians to form a group and put on a lunchtime show.

18. Set up sports teams to have friendly games with customers and trade partners.

19. The next best idea competition: Have teams compete for the next best idea.

20. Have an alter ego day: Dress up as the person you would most like to be, other than yourself.

SUCCESS HABIT FOUR: BE A "FIRST-GIVER"

The Law of Reciprocity

He almost didn't see the old lady stranded on the side of the road. But even in the dim light of day, he could see she needed help. So he pulled up in front of her Mercedes and got out and approached her. He could see that she was frightened, standing out there in the cold. He knew how she felt. "My name is Bryan; let me help you ma'am. Why don't you wait in the car where it's warm?"

Even with the smile on his face, she was worried, because he looked poor and hungry. All she had was a flat tire, but that was bad enough for an old lady. Was he going to hurt her?

Bryan crawled under the car looking for a place to put the jack, skinning his knuckles a time or two. Soon he was able to change the tire. As he was tightening up the lug nuts, she rolled down the window and began to talk to him. She was just passing through and couldn't thank him enough for coming to her aid.

Bryan just smiled as he closed her trunk. She asked him how much she owed him. Bryan never thought twice about the money. This was not a job to him. This was helping someone in need, and God knows there were plenty who had given him a hand in the past. He had lived his whole life that way, and it never occurred to him to act any other way. He told her that if she really wanted to pay him back, the next time she saw someone who needed help, she could give that person the assistance they needed. He added, "That's what we need in this world, is to help one another and pass it on."

He waited until she started her car and drove off. It had been a cold and depressing day, but choosing to help the old lady, made him feel good. A few miles down the road the old lady saw a roadside café. She decided to grab a bite to eat, and take the chill off. It was an old-style diner. Outside were two old gas pumps and inside it looked empty. The whole scene was unfamiliar to her. Her waitress came over and brought a clean towel to wipe her wet hair. She had a sweet smile, one that even being on her feet all day couldn't erase. The old lady noticed that the waitress was many months pregnant, but she never let the strain and aches change her attitude. She was friendly, polite, and patient, explaining each item on the menu.

The old lady wondered how someone who had worked all day could be so giving to a stranger. Then she remembered Bryan – that's twice in one day! While the waitress went to get her change, the old lady slipped out the door. Returning to the table, the waitress wondered where she could be, to her surprise, she noticed a note under which were four $100 bills. The note read "Please, accept this gift. Somebody helped me today and told me that what we need to do in this world, is to help one another. Don't let this act of kindness end with you – pass it on!"

That night when the waitress got home from work and climbed into bed, she was thinking about the money and what the old lady had written. How could the old lady have known how much she and her husband needed extra money? With the baby due next month, the $400 was a blessing. She knew how worried  her husband was, and as he lay sleeping next to her, she gave him a soft kiss and whispered, "Everything's gonna be all right; I love you, Bryan."

-Author Unknown

Only when you give of yourself, do you learn about the power you receive from giving. You receive elevated self-esteem, validation, and growth. Do not be afraid to give. You can never lose that which you give. If you are a kind person, it's impossible to lose your kindness. If you teach someone something, you still have what you taught them. Just give without expectation. The Dalai Lama says, "No one ever needs a reason to be generous and kind."

Being a first-giver means you believe in sharing and contributing, and not being a bystander. Being a first-giver builds pillars of empathy, understanding, and human connection. First-giving is nonmaterial. It is about wholeheartedly being dedicated to supporting a purpose, cause, or a shared destiny. Dedication is a powerful gift. You may be dedicated to your work, your church, your family, or to life in general. Dedication results in contributing positive energy, creative solutions, a good attitude, a soft face, and a great person to work with. As a first-giver, you manifest a universal law – the law of reciprocation. Some scientists call it the law of cause and effect: "every action has an appropriate reaction." Human nature is such that if you treat a person with kindness, you will receive kindness in return. Even the most ardent cynics will eventually relent and return kindness.

Give Unconditionally
Have no "Fear" of Loss

Give love and you receive love, give friendship and you receive friendship. Be dedicated to being the first-giver. Have no conditional thoughts about needing something in return. Know that giving is within itself the reward – a gift.

Of course, there are times when the stress of the world of work will not be conducive to giving – but a sensible person always weighs the odds, and the odds are greater if you practice first-giving.

Must we have a reason to help those in need? A kind spirit and a generous heart are like cool breezes on a hot summer's day. People do not care how much you know until they know how much you care. Kindness and generosity are important behavioral activities, because they are building blocks that bring us closer to the ultimate connecting point–that point of total harmony, complete connection of mind, body, emotions, and spirit. That is the ultimate synergism. That is when two can create three or greater.

Kindness of spirit sends a deeper message. It says to the person: You are a VIP in my life, a very important person. It says: Your existence helps me feel worthwhile, and I like myself more when I'm around you; you are worthwhile. Kindness, courtesy, and politeness are powerful self-esteem builders.

"Wherever you go, take a gift. It does not have to be a material gift. You can give love or kindness or just a loving presence."

-Deepak Chopra

Two Wolves

One evening an old Cherokee told his grandson about a battle that goes on inside people.

He said, "My son, the battle is between two 'wolves' inside us all. One is Evil. It is anger, envy, jealousy, sorrow, regret, greed, arrogance, self-pity, guilt, resentment, inferiority, lies, false pride, superiority, and ego. The other is Good. It is joy, peace, love, hope, serenity, humility, kindness, benevolence, empathy, generosity, truth, compassion, and faith."

The grandson thought about it for a minute and then asked his grandfather, "Which wolf wins?"

The old Cherokee simply replied, "The one you feed the most."

-Author Unknown

Give Motivation and Encouragement

Encouragement, positive reenforcement, and positive communication make teamwork work. We all enjoy compliments from our bosses, but we feel especially good when our coworkers tell us how good we are.

New team members need help in getting up to steam quickly. Become a team motivator. A team motivator does not necessarily have a title–they sense when to give; when to become a coach, a counselor, a teacher; they willingly show others how to be successful. Team motivators are workplace leaders and jump in and help others. They show them how to give by example and give them a character gift that lasts a lifetime.

Work competency and knowing how to do a job well is one of the foundations of great contribution and gives the gift of workplace trust. When your team knows you care, they'll care, and go the extra mile to make the impossible possible.

*When people care,
there's magic in the air!*

How do you encourage somebody? How do you motivate them? One way is to look for the things that they do well in their jobs and let them know that you've noticed their talents. Another way is to give compliments, but be very specific; otherwise, it can appear to be insincere: "You're so wonderful at your job" is too general, rather say: "The respectful way you handled that customer complaint, was very impressive. I liked the way you controlled the situation–well done!"

Not all of us are outgoing and gregarious. Some people don't know how to be team players. People hold back because of embarrassment, lack of assertiveness, or lack of confidence; but that doesn't mean they are uncommitted. Help them find their voice. Many times, you'll find that quiet people have really good suggestions but they won't offer them until encouraged to do so. People are different and it is this difference that makes them valuable for problem-solving and building a stronger diverse team dynamic. The last thing you need is for everyone to be the same.

Teamwork is valuable–group think is dangerous.

Angels, Once in a While

In September 1960, I woke up one morning with six hungry babies and just 75 cents in my pocket. Their father was gone. The boys ranged from three months to seven years; their sister was two.

Their dad had never been much more than a presence they feared. Whenever they heard his tires crunch on the gravel driveway, they would scramble to hide under their beds. He did manage to leave 15 dollars a week to buy groceries. Now that he had decided to leave, there would be no more beatings, but no food either. If there was a welfare system in effect in southern Indiana at that time, I certainly knew nothing about it.

I scrubbed the kids until they looked brand new and then put on my best homemade dress. I loaded them into the rusty old '51 Chevy and drove off to find a job. The seven of us went to every factory, store, and restaurant in our small town. No luck. The kids stayed, crammed into the car, and tried to be quiet while I tried to convince whomever would listen that I was willing to learn or do anything. I had to have a job. Still no luck.

The last place we went to, just a few miles out of town, was an old Root Beer Barrel drive-in that had been converted to a truck stop. It was called the Big Wheel. An old lady named Granny owned the place and she peeked out the window from time to time at all those kids. She needed someone on the graveyard

shift, 11 at night until seven in the morning. She paid 65 cents an hour and I could start that night.

I raced home and called the teenager down the street that baby-sat for people. I bargained with her to come and sleep on my sofa for a dollar a night. She could arrive with her pajamas on and the kids would already be asleep. This seemed like a good arrangement to her, so we made a deal. That night when the little ones and I knelt to say our prayers, we all thanked God for finding Mommy a job. And so I started at the Big Wheel.

When I got home in the mornings, I woke the baby-sitter up and sent her home with one dollar of my tip money–fully half of what I averaged every night. As the weeks went by, heating bills added another strain to my meager wage. The tires on the old Chevy had the consistency of penny balloons and began to leak. I had to fill them with air on the way to work and again every morning before I could go home. One bleak fall morning, I dragged myself to the car to go home and found four tires in the backseat. New tires! There was no note, no nothing, just those beautiful brand new tires. Had angels taken up residence in Indiana? I wondered. I made a deal with the owner of the local service station. In exchange for his mounting the new tires, I would clean up his office. I remember it took me a lot longer to scrub his floor than it did for him to do the tires.

I was now working six nights instead of five and it still wasn't enough. Christmas was coming and I knew there would be no money for toys for the kids. I found a can of red paint and started repairing and painting some old toys. Then I hid them in the basement so there would be something for Santa to deliver on Christmas morning. Clothes were a worry, too. I was sewing patches on top of patches on the boys pants and soon they would be too far gone to repair.

On Christmas Eve the usual customers were drinking coffee in the Big Wheel. These were the truckers, Les, Frank, and Jim, and a state trooper named Joe. A few musicians were hanging around after a gig at the Legion and were dropping nickels in the pinball machine. The regulars all just sat around and talked through the wee hours of the morning and then left to get home before the sun came up. When it was time for me to go home at seven o'clock on Christmas morning, I hurried to the car. I was hoping the kids wouldn't wake up before I managed to get home and get the presents from the basement and place them under the tree. (We had cut down a small cedar tree by the side of the road down by the dump.)

It was still dark and I couldn't see much, but there appeared to be some dark shadows in the car–or was that just a trick of the night? Something certainly looked different, but it was hard to tell what. When I reached the car, I peered warily into one of the side windows. Then my jaw dropped in amazement. My old battered Chevy was full to the top with boxes of all shapes and sizes. I quickly opened the driver's side door, scrambled inside and kneeled in the front facing the backseat. Reaching back, I pulled off the lid of the top box. Inside was a whole case of little blue jeans, sizes 2-10! I looked inside another box: It was full of shirts to go with the jeans. Then I peeked inside some of the other boxes: There were candy and nuts and bananas and bags of groceries. There was an enormous ham for baking, and canned vegetables and potatoes. There was pudding and Jell-O and cookies, pie filling and flour. There was a whole bag of laundry supplies and cleaning items. And there were five toy trucks and one beautiful little doll. As I drove back through empty streets as the sun slowly rose on the most amazing Christmas Day of my life, I was sobbing with gratitude. And I will never forget the joy on the faces of my little ones that precious morning.

Yes, there were angels in Indiana that long-ago in December. And they all hung out at the Big Wheel truck stop.

-Author Unknown

Give Full Attention and Be Present

The Baggage Tree

In retail, it's all about the experience! You need to be customer responsive, you need to have a smile on your face, be upbeat, present, and professional. However, it is not uncommon for staff members to bring their emotional baggage to work and dump it on co-workers and even with customers.

One of my clients remedied this problem by putting a "Baggage Tree" outside every one of her stores. She then called a company-wide staff meeting and explained the  purpose of the tree: "I care for you all, but the most important person in our business is our customer. It has come to my attention that some of you are losing sight of that and not paying enough attention to customer requests. I found out that a number of you are bringing your baggage to work and discussing it with each other instead of taking care of business.*

To help solve this problem, I've put a six-foot tree outside each of your stores. This is a symbolic tree: when you come to work, I want you to hang your baggage on the tree. You can pick it up there when you leave. Trust me, it will still be there. If you bring your troubled relationships, your boyfriends, your uncles and aunts, and any other situation that will distract you, you will disappoint me, your team, and more importantly, our customers. I don't want you to do that. Without the customer, we don't have a business. To "WOW" customers, you need to be present with them. When you are present, it is complementary and flattering and it allows you to hear points of view more clearly and solve problems quicker . . . and that's what makes the difference."

It's teamwork that makes the dream work!

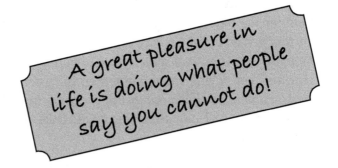

A great pleasure in life is doing what people say you cannot do!

Give by Being Competent

Teamwork requires individual responsibility and commitment for it to flourish!

Competency is the first and most important function of a high-performance team.

Great team players take 100% responsibility for their jobs and pay fanatical attention to detail (FAD) in everything they do. Competency requires a high degree of self-management and role responsibility, and is an important part of how high-performance teams build trust and achieve success. When each team member chooses to excel and direct their particular talent toward a shared destiny, it fosters a culture of respect which ripples out from internal to external customers.

You can go through life or you can go through life being your best!

Give Great Service to Internal and External Customers

A textile factory worker accidentally entangled himself in yarn. You can imagine what that was like. The more he tried to get out of it, the worse it got. Finally he yelled for help.

"Why didn't you call me before?" asked the supervisor.

"Well, I was trying to do the best I could on my own."

"The best you could've done was to call me. We're a team," said the supervisor.

When you call Company A, the person who answers the phone states the company name, her name, and the standard, "How may I help you?," but she speaks so quickly and in such a monotone, you can't understand a word she says. To confirm that you've called the right place, you ask, "Is this Company A?"

"Yes." The answer comes, but she doesn't elaborate, leaving you to pick up the conversational slack.

"Um . . . I'd like to ask a question about the gift baskets."

Silence. A sigh, by which the customer service

representative eloquently lets you know that you are making her life more difficult by your lack of organization and preparation. Then, that rapid-fire speech.

"Would that be the Incredible-Edible Gift Baskets, the Gift Baskets for Business, or the All-Candle and Cookie Selection?"

"Aah, could you tell me the difference between them? You see, I don't have a catalog, and . . ." This time, she cuts you off! "Is this for business, for friends, or for yourself?"

By now, you're irritated, because you're being treated like you're some kind of idiot and you're not getting the information you need. You want to know what's included in each basket, the cost, and the delivery options available for your time-line. But your customer service representative has a different agenda. Maybe she's tired, or someone was especially nasty to her, or they lost her paycheck, or she's worked two straight shifts. But it doesn't really matter what her problem is: What matters is that she's not really listening to you and she's not really talking to you. You might eventually get the answers you want from her and you might even place an order. But there's a good chance that the next time you need to order a gift basket, you'll look at another company, because this one left a bad taste in your mouth.

Now let's look at Company B. The phone is answered by a cheery-sounding person who takes the time to pronounce her words and inflect them like she's talking to a real person – you! When you ask about gift baskets, she carefully explains each basket, the contents and price, and she's enthused about the products. She asks how soon you want the basket delivered, and explains the delivery options. When you make a little joke, she laughs at it and sounds genuine. You come away from this interaction happy about your purchase, clear about when to expect delivery, and positive about the company from which you just ordered. You write down the phone number of Company B and put it in your database for the next time you need a gift basket.

We're all customers, and we're all, in one way or another, suppliers. Directly or indirectly, we supply customers with service or products, and frequently both. We are also all suppliers within our own companies. Payroll is a supplier to everyone in the company who draws a paycheck. Receptionists supply telephone calls and meeting information. Top managers supply other employees with training, role-modeling, career-building and motivation. No matter where you are in a company, no matter your job description, you are a customer of others in the company and a supplier to others in the company. The idea of customer service becomes a much grander concept when you realize that it's as important to be helpful to your coworkers as it is to be helpful to the external customers.

Under promise and over deliver.

For sales representatives and managers, internal customer service provides a reason for not promising (or implying) more than the rest of the company is able to deliver. When someone in sales promises a customer a fabulous discount for a top product in no time at all, those promises come back to haunt those in Accounting, Production, and even Shipping. In the end, something has to give: The external customer ends up angry and disappointed and the internal customers are stressed-out by trying to meet unreasonable demands. Maintaining good internal customer relations gives you the best chance of asking favors of your coworkers when you really need help pleasing the customer. Setting a company-wide standard of simple, straightforward rules of behavior ensures you'll have the best customer care without gimmicks.

"Out of difficulties grow miracles."

-Jean de la Bruyere

Give by Embracing Change

Be Prepared to Change!

Change is constant in the world of business. Alvin Toffler said, "Unless we can adapt and adjust to change, we're always going to be in a state of future shock." We need to be prepared for change and to change. We have to listen to other people's ideas, their points of view, and continuously modify the way that we do things.

Go as far as you can see; when you get there, you'll see further!

Mark Twain said, "Life is like being a river pilot on the Mississippi. What you learned yesterday, you have to relearn today." Business is a bit like that. Humanity's accumulated knowledge now doubles every 3 years. That means the rate of information and change is gaining momentum. We have no choice but to adjust, adapt, and learn. It is a new workplace, a new environment, and it requires new ways of thinking.

"I don't let my mouth say nothing my head can't stand."

-Louis Armstrong

Prisoners of Old Habits

It was Christmas and joy was in the air. The family were all gathered in the kitchen and the food was being prepared for the Christmas dinner. The group was made up of three generations, and it was good to see everyone so relaxed and at peace.

Roasting a large leg of lamb has been a family cultural tradition dating all the way back to when Grandma and Grandpa came to the United States. This year the youngest family member and newlywed, Jean, was hosting the Christmas dinner. As she was preparing the traditional leg of lamb, before putting it in the oven she cut off the lower shank of the leg– slid the rest into the pan and turned the oven to 350º, picked up her sherry, and noted with a voice of completion, "Well, that's it!"

"Wait a minute, Honey," said the new bridegroom. "Why did you cut the lower shank off the leg?"

Dumbfounded by the question, Jean responded, "I don't know, we've always done that in our family. Mom, why do we cut the lower shank off the leg of lamb?"

"I don't know, we've always done that in our family. I'm sure Grandma will know, she's in the living room."

Now on a mission, Jim, the son-in-law, approached Grandma respectfully. "Forgive me, Grandma, but I just noticed that Jean cut off the lower shank of the leg of lamb. She said that was a family tradition and so did Mom, who sent me to you to find out why the family does that?"

"Well, I don't know why Jean and my daughter would do that, but I did it when we first came to the USA because my baking pan was too small."

► Are you a prisoner of old habits?

► Do you do things over and over without questioning why?

► Are you limiting yourself by not embracing change?

See change as a source of
strength rather than a source
of stress.

*"They may forget what you said, but they
will never forget how you made them feel."*
-Carl W. Buechner

Give by Following the Golden Rule

Say "WOW" to the world and the world will say "WOW" to you!

The Golden Rule is the foundational principle of giving. It is grounded in the law of reciprocation. By having a willing attitude to first serve, internal and external customers will reciprocate by wanting to return the favor, respect and civility. It is integral to our nature as human beings. It's based on more than a win/win mentality–it's about first making others feel like winners. This is a shift in thinking away from the outdated idea that to win others must lose. It supports the idea that trust stems from reciprocal beneficial experiences. It's all about treating people in the way you would like to be treated.

"Tell me and I'll forget, show me and I'll remember. Involve me and I'll understand."

-Confucius

10 Ways to Live the Law of Reciprocity

1. Smile while greeting all internal and external customers. Give sincere compliments. Use people's names.

2. Be competent. Be trusted to do your part.

3. Be accountable and admit your mistakes. Fix mistakes and move on. Avoid ego defensiveness behavior.

4. Be candid and honest with everyone. Avoid diverting and game playing.

5. Embrace the idea of service–serve others first.

6. Communicate clearly and effectively. Speak clearly and have fanatical attention to detail (FAD).

7. Have a great attitude–be willing and coachable.

8. Be responsible–use your best judgement.

9. Be reliable–deliver on your promises.

10. Communicate effectively–listen actively. Talk less. Be polite and be FUN.

Give by Being a Professional

Fifty percent of our jobs are about what we do, the other 50% is about how we get on with others. Professionals in business take into account all the aspects of doing business. A professional is someone who takes their job seriously and willingly works with others to achieve company goals. Professionalism means that we take on the responsibility of creating goodwill among all team members at all levels of the organization.

"A pessimist sees difficulty in every opportunity; an optimist sees opportunity in every difficulty."

-Winston Churchill

Below is a list of everyday professional business manners and etiquette:

- ► Always greet and acknowledge everyone that enters your place of business.

- ► When being introduced to someone, have a firm handshake and make eye contact.

- ► Always be on time for meetings.

- ► Remember names and use them.

- ► Have good old-fashioned manners. Be polite.

► Allow people to finish saying what they want to without interrupting.

► Listen carefully, pay attention, be present.

► Know your company's policies, procedures, and products.

► Deal with customer and employee complaints immediately.

► Accept criticism graciously and make changes accordingly.

► Treat everyone equally.

► Work at understanding how others feel.

► Dress for success.

► Never discuss a staff member with another staff member.

► Be a high-performance team player.

► Always resign from a position graciously.

► Do not play win/lose games.

► Be open to suggestions.

► Be firm, fair, and fun.

► Be a straight-shooter.

Give by Being Innovative, Creative, and Finding Better Ways to Do Things

Contributing and moving the organization forward is everyone's responsibility particularly since everyone receives a paycheck. Job security, success, and job enrichment are all benefits that derive from choosing to be innovative and creative in the workplace.

Continuous improvement in every job and function leads to organizational transformation from good to great to world-class–and it all begins with each team player deciding to find new and better ways to do things.

Be ruthless with time and gracious with people!

Continuous education supports continuous improvement. Continuous education will open the door for team players to grow and develop, and become confident and well-groomed. Education is a fertility field for potential leadership. We need to take responsibility for helping our team players become more educated. Encourage individuals to attend training, and personally invest in training and education. Plant seeds that will give you fruit for the rest of your life.

The Results of Creativity

If you lived a 100 years ago . . .

► Your life expectancy would be 47.

► The average wage would be $200-$400 a year.

► A 3-minute telephone call from Denver to NYC cost $11.

► Most women only washed their hair once a month.

► The American flag only had 45 stars.

► The population of Las Vegas was 30.

► Only 6% of Americans graduated from high school.

► Antibiotics were not discovered yet.

► Ninety-five percent of physicians did not have a college degree–they attended a substandard medical school.

► The maximum speed limit was 10 mph.

Give Respect by Being on Time

Time is money . . . energy is money!

Stay on track and make sure you are on time for meetings, appointments, and delivery schedules. Being on time and keeping your appointments are integrity issues that speak directly to your level of professionalism and your ability to deliver on the commitments and promises you made.

Workplace happiness is a result of being a good time manager!

Time Management Tips

► Be disciplined and stay on track.

► Keep team players and visitors on track with an established agenda that covers time and topics.

► Always be polite, be friendly but firm about sticking to the agenda.

► Be ruthless with time but gracious with people.

► You have to teach people how to treat you.

- List no more than 6 priorities each day.

- Use gaps in the day for quick phone calls and to catch up.

- Remember time is money. Know how much it costs you to waste time.

- Energy is money. Time+energy=success.

- Do it today - don't procrastinate.

- Doing the right job makes you extremely effective. Doing the job right makes you efficient–do both.

- Know the difference between importance and urgency.

Don't let your lack of planning become my emergency!

"It has become dramatically clear that the foundation of corporate integrity is personal integrity."

-Sam DePiazza

Give Commitment to the Vision, Values, and Goals of Your Organization

"We hold these truths to be self-evident, that all men are created equal, that they are endowed by their creator with certain unalienable rights, that among these are life, liberty, and the pursuit of happiness."

-Declaration of Independence, July 4, 1776

When you are committed to the overall vision of the company, everyone around you can feel it. You become a motivator and energizer of the company culture. When team members believe in the vision, they become more secure. It gives everyone a greater sense of belonging. Building a successful company culture depends on how committed individuals and teams are to the vision, values, and goals of the company. Teamwork really is a value, not a training program. It is something that you believe in and are committed to. The workplace can be a place of great fulfillment and satisfaction for team members that willingly contribute on purpose.

Teamwork Values:

- ▶ Service
- ▶ Quality
- ▶ Attitude
- ▶ Respect
- ▶ Communication
- ▶ Responsibility
- ▶ Accountability
- ▶ Punctuality
- ▶ Competence
- ▶ Trust
- ▶ Professionalism
- ▶ Goal Achievement

Place high value on your work!

"He who asks the question may be a fool for five minutes, but he who never asks a question remains a fool forever."

-Tom Connelly

Give Your Voice to Ideas That Will Help the Team Move Forward

"Many of us are more capable than some of us . . . but none of us is as capable as all of us."

-Tom Wilson

Often, in meetings the loudest voice dominates and some of the best ideas are lost and forgotten. Individuals will hold back their opinions because they are unsure of how they will be accepted. When a team member holds back an opinion or a good idea, it neutralizes creativity and innovation and fosters a culture of non involvement. Never hold back your opinion or an idea–even if the company does not act on it. If you are shy, send your idea in by writing it out; or, if your company has a suggestion box, make use of it.

"Millions saw the apple fall–but Newton was the one who asked why."

-Bernard M. Baruch

An employee at the Kleenex Company was responsible for saving millions of dollars in labor by suggesting that the tissue boxes in hotel rooms be changed to have a base of colored tissues at the bottom of each box to warn room service teams that the boxes needed to be refreshed.

"You can never solve a problem on the level it was created."

-Albert Einstein

Southwest Airlines asked their staff members to find a way to avoid spending billions of dollars on new aircraft, and they delivered on that request by implementing a very simple idea: Turn the aircraft around quicker. The idea rested on how fast the staff could clean the planes and have them ready. That meant greater Synergy in-flight. Flight attendants would need to clean the planes in the air and quickly spot clean as passengers disembarked. Southwest staff members gave birth to an idea that not only saved billions of dollars but since then, has been adopted by many other airlines.

"We learn more by looking for the answer to a question and not finding it than we do from learning the answer itself."

-Lloyd Alexander

Many successes at Southwest are attributed to individual team players giving their ideas a voice and, thus, solving many daily problems.

Give by Valuing and Supporting Education

No matter what industry you are in today, education and training will give you a competitive advantage. The world is changing at such a pace that unless you are motivated and willing to stay current, you will be left behind.

Human beings have a natural tendency to resist change and gravitate toward the path of least resistance; unfortunately, that is also the path to obsolescence. You simply have to stay current with the technical advances in your industry. Set aside the idea that your job is only about what you have to do in today's workplace. It is also about relationships with your internal and external customers.

"You are never really playing an opponent. You are playing yourself, your own high standards, and when you reach your limits, that is real joy."

-Arthur Ash

A Voice for Education:

► A company is only as good as its people.

► If you think training is expensive, imagine what it would cost without it.

► People are only as good as they make their minds up to be.

► Ignorance is very expensive.

► People are motivated by growing their potential.

► No training, bad service, no profit.

► Customers love dealing with knowledgeable people.

► Training reduces the cost of sales and increases customer and staff retention.

"Make sure your team members know they are working with you, not for you."

-John Wooden

Give by Mentoring, Coaching, and Empowering Others: Pay it Forward

When to be a Teacher, Coach, Mentor and Counselor

Teacher: When team members are new and lack work experience, it is our responsibility to teach them how to do their jobs. When we are workplace teachers, we become workplace leaders, which supports the idea of continuous improvement.

"The harder I practice the luckier I get."
-Gary Player

Coach: The coach's role is to inspire and motivate team players to accomplish greater successes. A coach inspires accountability and dependability and is a nurturer of champions. Being a coach also means we have to be tough with ourselves and our teammates and insist on team discipline. A coach understands that morale and discipline are central to unity.

Mentor: Mentors are chosen by individuals who are searching for a sage, an advisor to help them in many areas of life. Mentors are generally excellent listeners and ask lots of questions. A good mentor is someone who helps a person find their own answers from within. Mentoring can be described as a guiding good friend who helps an individual clarify their own values, standards, and principles.

"The quality of a person's life is in direct proportion to their commitment to excellence, regardless of their chosen field of endeavor."

-*Vincent Lombardi*

Counselor: The counselor is an empathetic (not sympathetic) problem-solver. Empathy allows one to be objective and, therefore, be a part of the solution. Sympathy makes us a part of the problem. The counselor helps overcome problems by listening, guiding and asking pointed questions. This reveals a deeper understanding of the problem and way in which to come to a resolution. The counselor is like the pilot in a tugboat: showing the way, but not sailing the ship.

Give by Doing it Right First Time

Doing it right the first time saves energy, costs, and reputation, and makes the customer say "WOW!"

What is required to do this? Mostly a decision by you to approach every job with a sense of awareness, focus, and a determination to do the job with professionalism, confidence, and quality. It simply means you have to give your best effort to every job, making sure that you have checked and double-checked every aspect of the work you have done.

It means a steady and composed attitude that avoids nervousness and panicky actions that lead to mistakes. Avoid rushing jobs and focus on quality. More haste, less speed.

The High Cost of Getting it Wrong

- ▶ It costs about five times as much to get a new customer as it does to keep an existing one.

- ▶ Almost three out of four people think product and service quality are getting worse.

- ▶ Almost five times as many customers switch because of poor service and quality than price.

▶ More than 80% of customers say they'll stop dealing with an organization that doesn't meet their service and quality expectations.

▶ About 15% of customers stop buying a product because they're unhappy with it. Almost 70% stop because they think the company doesn't care.

▶ Sixty percent of people who get a positive response when they complain feel more confident about future dealings with a supplier; but 90% of customers feel negative reactions to complaints makes them feel less confident about future dealings.

▶ More than 50% of people who complain are dissatisfied with the response. More than 50% stop buying from the offending firm.

▶ Satisfied customers tell between 3 and 5 people about their experience; unhappy ones tell between 11 and 15.

▶ For every one complaint you hear, between 10 and 50 are unreported.

▶ It's outrageously expensive to ignore quality and service.

"Quality is remembered long after the price is forgotten."

-*Gucci Family Slogan*

Give Leadership by Example

Leadership is found at every level of an organization and begins with personal leadership!

Leadership has more to do with communication, influence, and showing the way. To lead does not mean to manage. Management suggests being in control to manage schedules, work flow, cash flow, and so on. To lead means to walk out in front and show the way. In a high-performance team, the leadership role goes to the person most competent in achieving the desired result.

Workplace leadership is common in high-performance teams because each individual is a leader within their speciality, within their core competence. Just as you should give your voice to the improvement of performance, give leadership guidance in the area in which you are most competent.

The single constant of success is good leadership!

"A leader is a dealer in hope."

-Napoleon Bonaparte

166

Kindness of a Stranger

It was a bitter, cold evening in Northern Virginia many years ago. The old man's beard was glazed by winter's frost while he waited for a ride across the river. The wait seemed endless. His body became numb and stiff from the frigid north wind.

He heard the faint, steady rhythm of approaching hooves galloping along the frozen path. Anxiously, he watched as several horsemen rounded the bend. 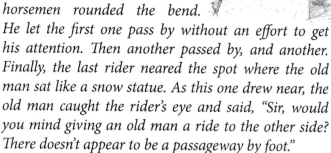 *He let the first one pass by without an effort to get his attention. Then another passed by, and another. Finally, the last rider neared the spot where the old man sat like a snow statue. As this one drew near, the old man caught the rider's eye and said, "Sir, would you mind giving an old man a ride to the other side? There doesn't appear to be a passageway by foot."*

Reining his horse, the rider replied, "Sure thing. Hop aboard." Seeing that the old man was unable to lift his half-frozen body from the ground, the horseman dismounted and helped the old man onto the horse. The horseman took the old man not just across the river, but to his destination, which was just a few miles away.

As they neared the tiny but cozy cottage, the horseman's curiosity caused him to inquire, "Sir, I notice that you let several other riders pass by without making an effort to secure a ride. Then I came up and you immediately asked me for a ride. I'm curious why, on such a bitter winter night, you would wait and ask the last rider. What if I had refused and left you there?"

The old man lowered himself slowly down from the horse, looked the rider straight in the eyes, and replied, "I've been around these here parts for some time. I reckon I know people pretty good." The old-timer continued, "I looked into the eyes of the other riders and immediately saw there was no concern for my situation. It would have been useless even to ask them for a ride. But when I looked into your eyes, kindness and compassion were evident. I knew, then and there, that your gentle spirit would welcome the opportunity to give me assistance in my time of need."

Those heartwarming comments touched the horseman deeply. "I'm most grateful for what you have said," he told the old man. "May I never get too busy in my own affairs that I fail to respond to the needs of others with kindness and compassion."

With that, Thomas Jefferson turned his horse around and made his way back to the White House.

-Author Unknown

I said, "Do you love me?" and she said, "No, but that's a really nice ski mask."

-Lloyd Christmas (Jim Carey) Dumb & Dumber

"Hello, this is Harris. I'm in right now, so you can talk to me personally. Please start talking at the sound of the beep."

-Harris K. Telemacher, LA story

Give by Being Courteous and Well-Mannered

Teamwork is all about relationship civility; and respectful good manners and courtesy are the lubricants for willing cooperation!

Team Courtesy Rules

1. Be Polite

In general, the rule is to do everything possible to enhance the cooperation and collaboration amongst one another. One nonnegotiable rule is courtesy. Children of several decades ago were taught to be polite as a matter of course, but that's no longer the norm, so companies now have to train employees in etiquette. Courtesy is contagious, and should be practiced by people at all levels of an organization. Courtesy is a social lubricant: When you find yourself in a sticky situation with a cranky customer, good manners will frequently help you move past arguments and on to effective problem-solving.

2. A Smile Is Worth a Thousand Words

Everyone is entitled to a courteous interaction, and one key interpersonal icebreaker is to smile when you talk to someone personally or on the phone. Smiling makes your voice lift and sound happy! Research has demonstrated that smiling also releases endorphins in your brain, causing you to actually feel happier.

> "A gentleman is one who never hurts anyone's feelings unintentionally."
>
> -Oscar Wilde

3. Speak Clearly

When you say the same thing 200 times a day, it gets to be monotonous really fast and becomes boring. It pays to understand that it's not monotonous for the person with whom you're talking! It may be the first time they hear you say something that you've said over and over, especially on the phone where there are no visual clues to supply the missing meaning. People can be totally in the dark if the person on the other end is going through the motions on auto-pilot. When you pick up the phone, take a breath, and speak slower than what comes naturally. If you are a presenter or salesperson, make sure that you are talking with your team rather than talking at them or just trying to get through it.

4. Listen

The greatest way to show respect for another person is to listen. Likewise, the best way to negotiate, to set goals, to make sales is to listen to your customer; and the best way to get along with your coworkers is to take the time to hear what they're saying to you. When you listen, shut out your own mental voice and concentrate fully on what the other person is saying. Put aside your own comments, doubts, and questions. If they're important, they'll come back to you later!

Listen with your whole self. Eighty-five percent of communication comes in non-verbals, so it's easier to really know what someone is saying when you can see each other. However, there are clues you can follow on the phone (e.g., pauses, repetitions, hesitations). Use your intuition and your empathy to tune into what the other person may be feeling while you are talking to them.

If you're not sure you understand what is being said to you, it's a good practice to repeat what you think is the gist of the message back to the other person, who can correct you if you're wrong, clarify a point, or agree with you if you're right. Some of the biggest messes can be avoided by checking in if you're not absolutely sure you know exactly what the other person is saying. Also, if you get the impression that someone hasn't heard your meaning, don't be afraid to go over it once again, more clearly.

5. Pay Attention to Diversity

Researchers have found again and again that men and women use language in different ways. Being brought up to express themselves more subtly than men, women tend to be more diplomatic in speech. A woman may phrase an order as a question, and a man may hear her making a suggestion rather than a demand. On the other hand, because they can be brutal in speech, men may sound like they're giving an order because most men are taught that directness is a desirable male attribute (i.e., it shows he really knows what he's after!).

Unfortunately, gender differences in speech can cause frustration, hurt feelings, and general confusion. No one way is better or worse than the other; it's just important to recognize that there are different ways of communicating.

Cultural diversity is also an important part of workplace communication: People from different cultures have different ways of behaving, different expectations, and different outlooks on life. When working with people from cultures different from your own, it's important to pay attention to preventing or repairing misunderstandings. There are books and seminars on inter-cultural relations and, especially in today's global climate, it makes good sense to become educated about the mores and norms in the cultures of the people with whom you work.

"A big man is one who makes us feel bigger when we are with him."

-John C Maxwell

"Don't say you don't have enough time. You have exactly the same number of hours per day that were given to Helen Keller, Pasteur, Michelangelo, Mother Teresa, Leonardo de Vinci, Thomas Jefferson, and Albert Einstein."

-H. Jackson Brown

Give by Practicing
Quality in All You do

Practicing quality is the adherence to and the practice of excellence within all the work that you and the team does. Accept nothing less than quality. Produce great quality if you're a printer. Bake the best cakes if you're a baker. Manufacture the best cars if you're an auto manufacturer!

How do you help to do that as a team player?

It's all in the way you think! When you think quality, you think: "This job is going to be the best job I have ever done." That kind of thinking will make you behave differently than when you think: "This is just another job." Commitment to anything in life starts with the way you think. Add the word "quality" to every thought and sentence you use and insist on greatness. As noted earlier, you develop greatness by having fanatical attention to detail (FAD), which requires that you spend time measuring everything you do. Make sure that you cross the t's and dot the i's- do it right first time.

The Reasons Why Quality Won't Work

► When people have hidden agendas and double standards.

► If you shoot the messenger of critical evaluation.

► If you support the few whiners, not in my back yard or in my department types— known as N.I.M.B.Y.s and the resisters of all change.

► If you believe your pocket is more important than quality. Quality is about building, growing, and developing something great!

► If you don't follow through and measure results.

► If you don't acknowledge problem areas. "Maybe it will fix itself"

► If you do not communicate your expectations of quality to your team.

► If you don't reinforce quality disciplines. Discipline means: coaching, teaching, focusing, directing, demanding, and challenging everyone to become world class.

► If you don't lead by example.

► If you do not become the driving force for quality.

Give Yourself the Gift of Giving

*"A bit of fragrance always clings
to the hand that gives roses."*

-Chinese Proverb

It is as important to know how to give as it is to receive. If we understand the principle behind "As you sow, so shall you reap," we will understand that whatever we give to someone is a gift to ourselves. Give love and we receive love; give friendship and we receive friendship but have no attachment to needing something in return. The principle is to give, unconditionally.

We must learn to give and receive gracefully and feel worthy of the gifts that flow forth. The gifts of life are so plentiful, but a sense of awareness is needed to recognize them. Mostly, the gifts of life are not materialistic. Nature provides so many of them: flowers in the spring, cool breezes on a warm summer's afternoon, a cozy fire to cut the cold of a winter's night, the colors of fall, a baby's giggle, the sound of laughter, a hummingbird's amazing aerial feats, waterfalls, cleansing rain, a rainbow, and a full moon–not to mention the gifts of touch, taste, smell, sight, and hearing.

What gifts have you been ignoring? Take the time to experience these gifts. You won't regret it. It may just open a whole new world for you.

The Joy of Giving:

▶ When we help others, it builds our self-esteem.

▶ When we give of ourselves, we teach others the value of compassion.

▶ When we give kindness and generosity, we break down hate and prejudice.

▶ When we give to the needy, we demonstrate our character.

▶ When we give, we create a force multiplier–a Synergy of giving.

▶ When we give, we contribute and serve others, and pay our rent for being on this planet.

▶ When we give, we open the door of reciprocity.

The more I give, the more I want to give.
The more I want to give, the more I find I have to give.
The more I find I have to give, the more I discover about myself!

20 Ways to Be a First-Giver

1. Give unconditionally. Have no "fear" of loss (i.e., to give without expectation of return).

2. Give motivation and encouragement to your team.

3. Give full attention and presence to those with you.

4. Give by being competent and doing a great job.

5. Give great service to internal and external customers.

6. Give by embracing change.

7. Give by following the Golden Rule: Treat others as you would like to be treated.

8. Give by making eye contact and listening.

9. Give by being innovative and creative, and find better ways to do things.

10. Give respect by being on time every time.

11. Give commitment to the vision, values, and goals of your organization.

12. Give your voice to ideas that will help the team move forward.

13. Give by valuing and supporting education and training.

14. Give by mentoring, coaching, and empowering others– pay it forward.

15. Give by doing it right first time.

16. Give leadership by example.

17. Give by being courteous and well mannered.

18. Give by practicing quality in all you do.

19. Give to those who are less fortunate.

20. Give yourself the gift of giving.

SUCCESS HABIT FIVE: BE A SYNERGIST

How Brian Lost His Synergy

Bill Martin was employed by Magic Products, a New York based consumer products distributor. Finally, his hard work paid off and he was promoted from National Sales Manager to Senior Vice President.

Magic Products' policy was to promote from within and Bill needed to find someone to fill his old position. His two prime candidates were Bryan Adams and George Abrams. So, Bill met with Bryan Adams in Los Angeles and gave him the good news. "Bryan, I have been promoted to Senior Vice President and I believe both you and George Abrams have the qualities to take over as National Sales Manager. This is very difficult *for me because you have both been with me since we started this division. So, the person who achieves the highest sales between now and the beginning of the financial year, six months from now, gets the job."*

Bryan exclaimed, "George Abrams does not stand a chance! I'm going to give you no alternative but to appoint me as the National Sales Manager. I have been waiting and working for this opportunity since I joined this company."

Bryan was excited as he drove home. He pictured himself in the new position. His excitement continued as he shared the events of his afternoon with his wife and children. That same evening he contacted all his field managers and instructed them to be in the office at 7:30 the next morning. He announced exactly what Bill Martin had told him, and he pointed out that if the team performed well, there would be a ripple effect of promotions throughout the Los Angeles branch.

Bryan was excited and inspired and his enthusiasm was contagious. He was in flow and his team caught the energy. Immediately, sales began to increase. July was a record month. August was even better, September outstanding; and October, November, and December were great months. This team was on fire, synergizing on all cylinders, and Bryan Adams was growing in confidence every day. According to the published data, Bryan would be the next National Sales Manager. The year ended well for the Los Angeles team.

In January, Bryan received an email from the Corporate Office requesting him to attend a special meeting in New York to announce the appointment of the new National Sales Manager.

"This is it - This is it! They're going to announce me as the new National Sales Manager." On his flight to New York, he was the epitome of enthusiasm, talking to everyone and generally enjoying himself and life. When he arrived at JFK, there was a company car waiting to drive him to the meeting. As he entered the lobby, the receptionist told him that Bill Martin wanted to see him before the big announcement.

Bryan thought, "Well, of course, Bill wants to see me. He wants to congratulate me and go over things before the meeting. He is a real gentleman."

With a confident stride, Bryan entered Bill's plush office. "Hello, Bill, how are you?"

Bill handed him a folder and said, "Bryan, I wanted to see you before the meeting because there is something really important that you should know."

Bryan opened the folder, which contained both his and George Abrams' sales figures in large colored graphs across the page. To Bryan's dismay, he saw that George had put in a huge order on the closing afternoon.

"Are you trying to tell me something, Bill?" Bryan asked.

Bill responded, "Now, Bryan, you know what the deal was."

During the meeting, Bryan switched off all awareness and felt numb all over. He went through the motions doing his best not to let on how angry he was. At the end of the meeting, Bill announced George Abrams as the new National Sales Manager.

Everybody wished him well, except Bryan. He felt an overwhelming sense of betrayal, anger, and resentment and immediately left for the airport.

As he got off the plane in Los Angeles, his wife detected immediately that he had not gotten the job.

As they walked toward their car, she asked, "You didn't get it, did you?"

Bryan looked at her and said in a sarcastic tone, "Do me a favor, I don't want to talk about it!"

She felt hurt. A dark cloud hung over their drive home.

Once home, Bryan fell into a depression. He didn't feel like doing anything or seeing anyone, including the children.

At work, Bryan kept to himself, resisting participation in meetings and company functions. During the following months, his attitude negatively impacted his work, his team, and sales; attitudes and motivation became progressively worse. In a strange way, Bryan secretly felt a sense of satisfaction, almost revenge. He became more and more cynical and demotivated.

Two months later, George Abrams, the new National Sales Manager, flew to Los Angeles and fired Bryan Adams.

What Happened to Bryan?

He fell into one of life's lesson plans. All of us have had to deal with life's lessons at one time or another. We have all experienced emotional battering from a job, relationship, or one of many other difficulties. We have all been knocked down at one time or another. What's important is how we deal with it, how we roll with the punches.

Bryan wouldn't roll with the punches. Mentally and emotionally he lost his objectivity and became reactive. Wrong thinking made him become bitter and he went into a downward spiral of negativity, the 3R Syndrome:
Resentment, Resistance, Revenge.

Resentment

When our expectations aren't fulfilled, valid or not, we resent it. In Bryan's case, the expectations were valid and his disappointment was very real. Right when he suffered his loss, Brian needed to exercise a right thinking choice before he reacted negatively. He resented not getting the job and his pride was hurt when he overheard his colleagues feeling pity for him. He felt empty and betrayed. He wondered why he should be trying so hard. The resentment he felt acted as a poison, causing him to act childishly by not congratulating his opponent. Then it followed him home, where he hurt his wife's feelings and ignored his kids.

The most painful things in life are rejection and isolation. When Bryan didn't get the job, he felt rejected by the company he worked for. His reaction was to draw away, further isolating himself from his coworkers and his family, and increasing his unhappiness. For someone who is unbalanced, who has been rejected and isolated throughout life, a situation like the one Bryan faced could have easily manifested into violent retaliation. As it stood, Bryan lost face at work, lost any enthusiasm he once had for his job, and lost a precious hunk of his self-esteem.

Resistance

Resistance and closing down is a way to psychologically run away from a problem. It's an expression of anger when we can find no other outlet. In Bryan's case, resistance manifested itself as a sort of personal 'get-you-back' sabotage. He stopped caring about his work and endeavored to get his work group to join him.

Resistance as a nonviolent opposition strategy works wonderfully well, and was used pro-actively by Ghandi and Martin Luther King. Someone who's practicing purposeful physical passive resistance, is extra heavy, floppy, and difficult to move. But daily unplanned, passive aggressive resistance is rarely useful as a way of influence, because it lacks a positive synergistic focus. It's totally self serving. It tends to create an emotional boomerang of negative re-actions. The relationship becomes stuck unable to effectively make the very change needed. When Bryan was resisting the acceptance that he had lost the job he'd dreamed of, he could have made a new plan, come up with the 'right' choices. One of those choices could have been to find a new job,this is not uncommon, a fresh start would allow him to regain his motivation and sense of self worth. Another choice might entail staying with the company and keeping his sales high. This would position him well for future promotions. He might have negotiated a bigger bonus for himself and his group based on the last 6 months' sales. He got lost in grieving over the job he didn't get, and it hurt him much more than it hurt the large company he worked for.

Bryan's internal monologue reflected what was tormenting him. It was full of revenge, so that in his head he was saying, "I'll get you back for this," and "If you can't treat me well, I won't even try." He was talking to Bill and George and anyone who he imagined had something to do with his loss. It was all classic passive aggressive emotional turmoil. Unwittingly Bryan was punishing himself, because his subconscious was listening to his angry pronouncements and acting to help perpetuate his feelings.

Sometimes we get into the 3R's because we are scared to stand up for ourselves. Passive-aggressive behavior comes directly from feeling unable to be open about anger. Your partner does something stupid and thoughtless, but instead of saying, "Hey, you hurt my feelings", you bite your lips because nice people aren't supposed to get angry (an interesting idea passed down by generations of passive-aggressive ancestors). But a single lip-bite won't do, because the original hurt starts to fester, and soon there are a dozen other small but irritating issues. You start to think vengeful thoughts, and the passive-aggressive stuff starts, maybe with the silent treatment.

If you're mad at someone, it's so much easier to tell them, why and wait for an apology. State your case. Say "no" when you want to say no. Feel free to disagree, and if you were taught as a child that it's bad to disagree, it's time to let go of that mistaken idea.

Revenge

Bryan tried to get even with Bill Martin by not maintaining the terrific growth of his branch. He did not attend meetings. He closed his door and was slow to return calls. He was generally defensive and rude. The greatest revenge of all he took was against himself. His feelings of failure about himself generated a self-fulfilling prophesy and an outward attitude that was intolerable to others. Bryan was fired, and it was a wake-up call for him. He reassessed his life, his purpose, and his goals. He made changes to the way he was thinking and acting. Today, Bryan is very successful with another company.

The **3R's** can be counteracted by the **3A's**. Replace Resentment, Resistance, and Revenge with Awareness, Attitude, and Action for a successful answer to these kind of challenges.

How Bryan Got His Synergy Back!

Awareness

Bryan learned that greater personal awareness was the first step to getting out of the 3R's. He became aware of how he talked about his angry feelings: "I just blew up", "I went ballistic", and "I lost it". He recognized how important it is to notice how you feel before you get angry.

Usually hurt, fear, or shame come before anger–either one at a time or all at once. Anger is the follow-up feeling that distracts you from the others, which are more painful. Awareness of the feelings underlying anger will tone down outbursts and allow you to focus on getting your needs met. It is all about finding ways to co-create Synergy. At work it can be as simple as redirecting negative energy and working together to load up a truck with your teammates or as complicated as learning a new computer program. It's all about being aware, choosing to have the right mental attitude and having a willingness to be the first-giver.

Bryan recalled how he ignited the energy and awareness when he created the high-performance team at Magic Products. He realized that when you come to work, you must have a sense of awareness of everything around you. Be present, be ready to connect, sense and feel everything.

Know your work environment. Be aware of how your personality affects other team players and look for areas of understanding and agreement rather than disagreement. Bryan learned that people relate to you better if you have an attitude of cooperation and self-control.

Attitude

Right mental attitude (Success Habit Two: RMA) influences everything! It's difficult to stay positive when you've had a major disappointment like Bryan's, but the payoffs make it worthwhile. Take time to digest unpleasant events and plan ways to make the best of them. Ask yourself what you can learn from your experience. Use visualization techniques such as a mental movie screen to project positive outcomes. Change your thoughts and reactions by changing the pictures in your mind. Practice faith, believe that you can and will find solutions for your situation. Even in the toughest times, be gracious with others, and yourself.

It took getting fired for Bryan to realize that his thoughts influenced his feelings and in turn his actions. Right thinking leads to right actions.

It is, what it is!

Action

Right actions are always grounded in the best intentions. Correct actions are the product of right thinking and are designed to improve the quality of our businesses, our lives and the lives of those with whom we work.

Admitting mistakes, showing responsibility, and being accountable for situations and over-sights in judgement are always the correct actions. These actions help relationships maintain trust going forward. To avoid the 3R's, actions may include damage control such as letting go of envy and resentment, e.g., congratulating business competitors, and apologizing and moving on. Do not over-obsess about something that cannot be changed. After the fires are all out, learn from the experience and turn a crisis into a gain. There is almost nothing in the world of relationships that cannot be repaired–if addressed with honest intentions and actions.

Show me the Synergy!

Attitude

Awareness

Right Thinking

Action

The Synergy Experience

You've probably had the experience of being totally involved in an activity that takes high levels of your concentration and skill. You might have been painting, singing, writing, completing a special work project, or immersed in the development of a new product, but the feeling was the same–pure enjoyment, deep satisfaction, and the sensation that time stood still. When you did finally look at the clock, you were amazed at how the hours flew by. This unique peak experience has been researched and documented by Mihaly Csikszentmihalhyi (*Flow: The Psychology of Optimal Experience*) and is aptly called "being in flow," which is the perfect description of a Synergy experience. When you are in "flow," the world feels right and perfect. You are challenged but not frustrated, wholly immersed in the experience and glad to be where you are. You wouldn't trade this experience for anything else!

When your mind, body, emotions, spirit, and actions are all engaged in a single purpose, the feeling is exhilarating; it's a high no drug can ever match. When you look back on a Synergy experience, you might see it as a miracle, an aberration, or something that only happens once in a blue moon. In fact, when you consciously focus on Synergy in your everyday life, you increase the number of peak flow experiences, and you increase their duration. Like any skill, the more you practice Synergy, the better it will work for you. Use Synergy daily, and "day-to-day" will come to mean what it really should: daily opportunities to multiply your success, job fulfillment, and well-being.

When you think synergistically and work as a team, you don't rail against misfortune, argue with one another, or compete for recognition; you elevate your creativity and motivation. You make better individual and team decisions and implement more effective solutions that allow you and your team to be in flow.

It's important to think of Synergy not only as a natural phenomenon found in nature, but as something magical you can create. You have the capacity to make it happen continuously, at work, at home, and in every part of your life. All you have to do is adopt the five success habits detailed in this book, and the rest will follow naturally.

When a team is focused on a shared destiny, the improvement in productivity and problem solving ability becomes phenomenal.

Team Experiences

"We just clicked!" "Time flew by!" "We're on the same page!" "We were in the zone!" This is what people say about each other when they experience Synergy. In the same way that using your body, mind, and spirit together helps you achieve greater goals, working in a cooperative, intuitive, mutually sustaining relationship with someone else brings you terrific satisfaction and outstanding results. Much of what has been written about teamwork in the workplace is based on the idea of Synergy–when two or more people wholeheartedly act in concert to achieve a common goal.

When Synergy happens, it's a thing of beauty!

Therefore 1+1 may equal more than 2–it may equal 3 or more. When it comes to work, it means that if 1 person takes 4 jaw-clenching hours to complete a task, 2 people may complete the task in a much shorter time. Four people can get the job done in about 35 minutes, and it will be less stressful and the accomplishment rewarding. Adam Smith, considered by many to be the father of free enterprise, explains it best in his example of the division of labor. He used the making of pins to point out the benefits of combined effort towards a common goal. "One worker could make 20 pins a day, but 10 workers dividing the 18 steps required to make a pin, could make a combined total of 48,000 pins a day." A team that has Synergy can accomplish more than larger groups or even more skilled groups where Synergy isn't part of the process. When there is Synergy, everything flows, creativity is rampant, people cooperate to create the best solutions, and everyone's having a great time.

Volunteer projects are a good place to experience Synergy. If you've ever taken part in a community project such as cleaning up a beach or park, you may have felt what it's like to work with a group of people making a plan, visualizing the goal, encouraging each other on to success, and celebrating afterwards. It is much like the flow experienced by individuals, but the achievement is larger–after all, two dozen people can repaint a church in a weekend, but one person might take a solid month.

The other payoff of Synergy is the relational aspect of it–anytime you co-create Synergy with other people, you are making friends, building trust and respect, and having fun–activities most people sorely need.

Synergy Always Works from the Inside Out

Choosing to learn and grow from each experience and improve your personal performance is a part of the Synergy philosophy. It is choosing life and growth over inertia and decay. It is choosing to discover more of our hidden talents and potential, and it is a healthy way of life. The more we discover, the more we create a foundation of self-worth. Honoring and respecting ourselves is vital because our relationship with ourselves becomes the greatest force we have. Once we're winning inside, it's easy to feel secure with others and it's easier to communicate effectively.

All communication begins with ourselves. If our self-esteem is low, we may even choose to set ourselves up by constantly complaining about how little we have, and how much others have. This is the "victim" game. They're rich, they're lucky, they're talented. They have it all and I have nothing. This kind of thinking is poisonous and leads to negativity, apology, suppressed anger, frustration, and passive aggressive communication. This is a major source of envy and can create verbal violence, and the 3R's-resentment, resistance, and revenge. 3R's lead to many physical and mental illnesses and, oftentimes, horrific workplace violence. Establishing a sense of purpose and working with others toward personal and collective goals is the right way to feel validated.

Synergy Triple-Win

Triple-win is a leadership force multiplier: Employees win by working for leaders who are committed to the principle of service. They have clear vision and the emotional maturity to recognize that leading is about bringing out the individual talents of each team member. They are passionate energizers, coaching and focusing the combined talents of the team toward a predetermined shared destiny. In this way, employees win, the company wins, and the customer wins. It is service from the inside out. Employees who are well-trained engaged and empowered and have job satisfaction are more invested in educating and giving customers exceptional service, who will reward the company with continued loyalty. Building a community of loyal customers in this way is a good reason for seeing your training dollars as an investment rather than an expense and a drain on profits. It's a simple yet powerful way to build a high-performance customer-driven culture from the inside out.

Choose the Higher Path

Synergy is ethically based because it takes all players into consideration and is focused on transparent communication, growth, and a triple-win mentality. It is a positive, intelligent strategic 'right' choice and will move any project upward and onward. To practice Synergy as a team player, you need to be emotionally secure and confident about what you can contribute–and what you need to do to make your 1(one) plus the 1(one) from the team, multiply into 3(three), or more. Our individual contributions become meaningful and respected based on three important ethical principles:

▶ Communicate with integrity.

▶ Practice a willingness to find mutually beneficial resolutions to problems and situations.

▶ Choose to be personally committed to the principle of continuous improvement.

The outcome from connecting mentality and creativity is fun, stimulating uncommon success!

This is a sharp departure from the way in which many people think and behave in the workplace. Many believe that it's all about winning–getting mine before others do. This a cynical and negative approach to work and to life. In my many years of working with people, I've noticed that this approach makes for untold amounts of stress-related conflicts and is a fundamentally flawed line of thinking. It is flawed because it takes huge amounts of energy (mostly negative) to defend oneself against, in many cases, imagined enemies. Of course there are people and companies who are rotten to the core, with negative politics and dishonest executives, who advocate a dog eat dog culture. Mostly they fail. No organization has the ability to cope with this kind of attitudinal cancer for long. It spreads rapidly and is like the "Trojan Horse" computer virus. It infects and interferes with everything and slows down the entire enterprise, creating even greater fear, de-motivation and destructive competition.

When we have a balanced philosophy and are willing to find the right way to interact with others, we build deeper trust and respect!

Workplace competitiveness is, for many, the basis of validating oneself, competing to be heard. Workplace competitiveness without focusing on a shared destiny separates individuals rather than connects them. It is based on a winner-takes-all mentality, which divides and weakens team unity. Undirected competitiveness brings about emotional insecurity and dissipates the focus of the team. It's just not smart business!

The smart way is to direct competitiveness and energy in an exciting, fun, and energizing way. Executed the right way, directed fun competition creates just the right amount of actionable tension and emotional security, rather than stress and anxiety. This happens when each team member is encouraged to align personal goals with company goals. There is nothing more powerful than a passionate team of people, aligning their goals with the company mission: It's the energy source of a business. In this way, team members feel free to clarify a point of view and allow it to be questioned, compared, discussed, and analyzed with a sense of objectiveness, oneness, and enjoyment. It's becomes you and me, against the problem, looking for the solution, rather than you and I competing against each other to come up with the solution first, which is a waste of income-producing energy!

Finding Your Talents for
Personal Synergy

My geographer friend is academically and socially intelligent. He knows what's important to other people and strives to make other people feel good when they're around him. His social intelligence has helped him build a career that spans the globe along with a personal life that is rich and filled with meaning. As discussed in my personal development book: *Creating Extraordinary Joy* and Success Habit Two of this book, there is more than one kind of intelligence: It's particularly important for team players to understand that individuals have different types of intelligence, and that it's vital to focus talent and intelligence on the right job. An academically intelligent person can learn and retain information easily, but his poor social skills may inhibit his career and ability to work synergistically with others. Someone who has a real genius for leading business meetings may have the physical grace of a raging hippopotamus. Individuals have their own unique contributions and it's important that these particular gifts are discovered, accepted, and dovetailed to create a strong seamless team. Naturally, there are people who are highly intelligent in more than one life area; and the more you develop various abilities, the more well-rounded and effective you will be at your job and within the team.

Authenticity is Key

Making authentic choices about what you're good at and like to do, and knowing that there is a place for your unique brand of smarts, is essential to your confidence and contribution to the team. In choosing a career, some people let their parents tell them what they're going to be, and never consider doing anything else. Unless you happen to be perfectly suited for what your parents want you to be, in career-counseling circles, this is called "foreclosure," you just opted out of the right to choose your own career path. The choices that turn out to be good for you must be based on who you really are, the needs and talents of your true self. Even if your talents mean you won't ever be a trial lawyer or a neurosurgeon, if you follow your natural strengths, you will be an excellent photographer, cabinetmaker, teacher, or CEO.

Connection is a Primal Need

Our jobs tend to be technical, detail-driven, and solitary. Our culture places great value on having plenty of individual space. We can watch TV alone, and we often don't know our neighbors, except for the polite greetings when we see them on our way to work. We move away from our families. We say we like it that way! Yet, we know connection with other people is a primal need, we need to be validated and need to know we have worth to ourselves and others. We often deny ourselves the time for deep connection by comparing relationships to time. This is an odious comparison. Good relationships are timeless. We will tell ourselves we just don't have the time and energy after a hard day at the office. Yet, in my ongoing workshops people tell me and write to me frequently about their loneliness and need for human connection.

Here is an email sent to me by a successful executive.

Subject: What do you Suggest?
To: "Chris Alexander" <calexander@synergyteampower.com>
Date: Saturday, October 27, 1:09 PM

Chris,
When you talked today about Synergy and need for connection, I felt you were talking to me.
I've been lonely since childhood, so I've almost gotten used to it. I don't tell anyone at work about this, because I learned early that being lonely means I'm weak, needy, and unlovable-maybe even weird. I convinced myself that other people don't feel this emptiness; they are strong. I don't want anyone to know these things about me. I can cope. I enjoy a few drinks with the guys at the local and it helps, but mostly, since the breakup of my last relationship, I watch TV, or spend hours on Facebook or Twitter, which lets me vicariously experience family life without having to actually live it.
The Internet allows me the perception that I connect with other people: I can log in and chat, I can look at other people's pages, people can text me when I'm away from home, and my staff can get me 24/7. And many do. But I'm still lonely. I would love to synergize with others.
What do you suggest?

The loneliness in our culture is so accepted, we don't even notice it anymore. We have come up with excuses for loneliness –we work harder and longer than other cultures (actually achieving no more than they do), we are "independent" and "free." We farm our children out to day-care and our parents to the old folks' home and return to an empty apartment each night bedraggled from work and empty of personal satisfaction. To achieve meaning, we have to express the true self, but expressing the self means there needs to be someone there to perceive us, react to us, synergize with us. In short, for me to express my true self, I need you.

Not recognizing the importance of Synergy in the workplace is like neglecting to fill up your vehicle with gas, and somehow still expecting to get to your destination!

Friends and Enemies of Synergy

Friends of Synergy

From the general atmosphere and attitude of a great workplace to the people I meet and admire and want to spend time with, the qualities that allow for Synergy to manifest tend to be the same:

A cooperative trustworthy environment, open shared communication, positive attitudes, respect, equality, innovation, fun, creativity, challenging work, and good leadership with a clear vision, clear values, clear goals, and clearly communicated expectations.

Enemies of Synergy

The mind-sets and behaviors of people in workplaces that inhibit Synergy also inhibit the ability for teams to interact effectively and dramatically reduce the potential for extraordinary results:

Dictator-style leadership, critical, competitive win-lose culture, overworked stress-filled atmosphere, lack of respect, secrecy, terrorist bosses, hostile inexperienced and weak leadership, too structured, too demanding, too strict, too routine, plodding, ambiguity, or totally unstructured and chaotic.

The Friend of Synergy is Right Thinking

Right Choices

You've been driving all day and half the night, and you haven't eaten since breakfast. Ravenous, you walk into a restaurant and the waiter hands you the menu. When you open it, you discover it contains only one item; a cheese sandwich. You don't want a lousy cheese sandwich! You want meatloaf and mashed potatoes and fruit salad and cheesecake (you're impervious to cholesterol)! But this is the only restaurant open in Fargo, North Dakota, at 10:00 on a Wednesday night. Then the waiter confirms that the one choice is all you have. So you sigh heavily and say, "I'll have the cheese sandwich."

Ultimately, you go away feeling gypped and unsatisfied. Because you weren't really free to choose, were you?

Going through life with one set of choices is like eating a cheese sandwich every day of the week because you never got to see the whole menu. Who we are, what the world is like, how other people see us are concepts we acquire by the time we're 5 years old. We learn from our families what the world is like, but we only learn about what our family-world is like. The outside world has so many other items on the menu! The challenge is saying to yourself, "Okay, when I was five (or six or ten), and living in the world my family created, I would have reacted this way. But I'm not a kid anymore, and I live in the whole world. What other choices are available to me?" Making a decision to connect in a larger way will be a force multiplier in your life. What you think influences how you feel and that will determine how you act.

Right Thinking

As I mentioned in Success Habit One, the phrase "right thinking" comes from Buddhism, and is one of the moral precepts of that philosophy. Right thinking is about holding your mind in a correct place in terms of what you believe; paying attention to your values. It's about practicing honesty and integrity when you're the only person at the table who is abiding by his principles, even when it might be more convenient or comfortable to forget. It might mean taking a loss to right a wrong. Staying focused on what matters most to you is crucial for your happiness. There may be all sorts of incentives to abandon your values, but the greatest incentive is the one we strive for here–an integrated life. When you stick with what you believe, your self-respect is intact, and although others may not agree with you, they will respect and trust you. You may be the only person who knows when a choice you make is "right" rather than "smart," but you will know; and it affects how you see yourself and the world.

An example of doing "right" instead of "smart" can be applied even to financial dealings. Say you have to make a choice between mutual funds. One carries the standard choices of oil and gas companies, mining interests and tobacco companies. Historically, this fund does quite well and the outlook for it in the current political climate is good, as the new President makes changes to support industry, turns government lands over to logging, and prepares to fund drilling in the Arctic. You could make some good money with this fund.

The second fund is almost as successful as the first, but it's longer term, depending on alternative energy companies, products from conservation-managed rain forests and cruelty-free cosmetic companies. This fund has proven to be a good steady bet, but it doesn't have the "get-rich-quick" status of the first one.

Doing right in this case, means looking at more than how much money you can make. What some might consider the "smart" choice might put out quicker profits, but at an added cost to the environment, increased burden on the health-care system and the heavy price of lung cancer spread across the generations. You can do right by thinking long-term and thinking of the larger consequences and taking personal responsibility for the real costs, which in this case is being smart as well. Synergy is the right choice to improve the quality of your personal, family and business life-it's also the smart choice.

When you choose what's right, you are automatically doing what's smart. Be warned, it may not be considered smart by those who equate "smart" with self-promotion at all costs. Whenever you go with your intuitive understanding of what's right, you are living from a deeper more considerate, yet broader view of the relationship with yourself, others, and life.

In Synergy, right thinking is also about making a choice to be positive whenever possible. This is a tall order, since we are often surrounded by cynical people who equate "optimism" or "positiveness" with being pollyanna and soft. Nothing could be further from the truth.

After all, in a world as troubled as ours, it's only natural to be pessimistic, right? Wrong! No right outcome can come from wrong thinking! How about this idea instead: Everything in life is about the choices you make; why not choose to be optimistic? Your odds are much better with optimism! Have you considered the consequences of negative thinking? Fear is the result of negativity and it robs us of hope, the very essence of life. Daily miracles may not make the six o'clock news, but just look around! Growth is everywhere! We can choose to grow even in the face of great despair and loss. The beauty of life is more than things and material gain.

The human spirit is extremely resilient and the survival instinct is increased exponentially through optimism and thwarted by negativity. All you have to do is break free; yes, free yourself from the pain of cynical negative projection and see the world around you. Babies are born, flowers bloom in the spring, snowflakes are perfectly constructed. Getting back to nature is one way to connect with a positive attitude, to recapture some of the magic you knew as a child.

Remember how excited you felt when you played and had fun, when you used your imagination to create magical visions, how excited you became when it snowed? When was the last time you ran out into the snow and made a snow angel, had a snowball fight, sculpted something really magnificent using only your mom's favorite spatula and your own creative genius?

It's never too late to have a happy childhood. All the qualities of your once optimistic child (e.g., curiosity, spontaneity, excitement, energy, honesty) are the ones we need for teamwork, good relationships, and the Synergy that manifests from living that way.

Optimism has lost its chic in contemporary culture, but that can change! In *Anatomy of an Illness*, Norman Cousins showed us that thinking positively, laughing often and hard can literally save our lives. Positive thinking is a vital part of living, and a requirement of the kind of Synergy we want to create in our workplaces. Synergy needs food to allow it to grow, and that food is optimistic mind-sets.

If you're thinking, "Oh, I couldn't possibly become an optimist at this late stage," this book is perfect for you! That thought, like all our thoughts, is a habit, and habits are made to be changed. Often, changing a habit is a matter of making a firm, committed decision to do one small thing today and another small thing tomorrow. Start changing the negative thinking habit right now.

When you find more positive ways to look at situations that have previously been uncomfortable, you are expanding your range of possible choices and increasing your chances for better relationships and growth.

Right Actions

Persistence is the essence of changing negative thought habits! Expect to challenge and change any one negative thought 20 times a day. Remember when you first started driving, and it seemed you would never learn all the rules, all the road signs, and the quirky shifts of the car? But soon, it was easier, and now it's automatic.

Changing your thoughts is like learning to drive–you are acquiring a new set of skills, which you will build into a new habit: A habit that will empower you and make you happier. So, keep at it. Take baby steps: Success is just around the corner!

Inch by inch, it's a cinch!

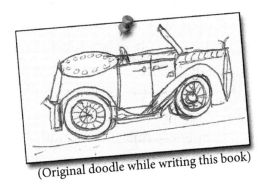

(Original doodle while writing this book)

The Enemy of Synergy is Wrong Thinking

With the human capability to form habits, we can create fixed thought patterns that influence our emotions and, in turn, our reactions when attempting to communicate with others. Wrong thinking projects negative behavior that distances relationships, exactly the opposite to what we want to build Synergy. Below are several wrong thought patterns and their right thinking antidotes. Which ones do you find cropping up in your life again and again? From which ones are you free? Which ones would you like to give up?

Silo-thinking

There is an unseen destroyer of communication, teamwork, and productivity. This destructive force lurks in every department and is ever present in the minds of managers, supervisors, and staff – at every level. It's called "the silo mentality," and is derived from the farming industry because farmers build silos to warehouse and protect their harvest. Silos are good for farmers – but silo mentality in the workplace is extremely dangerous, infectious, and expensive. Silos hinder communication, reduce innovation, limit problem-solving ability, and build walls instead of bridges.

A person with a silo mentality focuses solely on their specific job to the exception of their departments and company mission. Silos are created in organizations where there is a lack of trust and individuals feel they need to protect themselves. They feel insecure about jobs and therefore have a need to build a 360-degree "wall of protection."

In today's highly competitive world, a company cannot afford to have managers and staff with silo mentalities. Breaking down walls and building bridges between departments and job functions is a fundamentally sound strategy that pays off handsomely by reducing costs and speeding up production and service to customers.

The Synergy Antidote: How you build bridges and break down silo walls:

- ▶ Build trust.

- ▶ Have the right mental attitude.

- ▶ Be a first-giver.

- ▶ Fun is the great connector. There is nothing more enjoyable than working with people who have made their minds up to have fun at work.

- ▶ Be a problem-solver.

- ▶ Be respectful, courteous, and polite.

- ▶ Listen twice as much as you talk.

- ▶ Attend meetings and training seminars with an open mind. Everything on earth, including humanity, is either growing or decaying. The moment you think you know it all is a moment of decay.

- ▶ Be accountable for your actions and take full responsibility for your role in the team.

- ▶ Recognize that synergizing all jobs and all departments is important to the success of everyone in the organization; practice a philosophy of "triple win."

Conclusion Jumpers

Chicken Little is a storybook hen who was convinced that the sky was falling. She ran to everyone she knew, screaming that the heavens would soon be crashing heavily onto their heads. The sky never did fall, but Chicken Little had to start taking anti-anxiety drugs and was in therapy for years.

Sylvia's Sad Story

Sylvia was a conclusion-jumper, and she invariably assumed the worst. When her boyfriend invited her to dinner at the nicest restaurant in town, she became immediately apprehensive. She called her sister, wailing into the phone.

"Bob's taking me to Chez Panisse Saturday night," she moaned. "He's going to dump me, I can feel it." Her sister tried to console her, but Sylvia didn't listen to her. She stood Bob up that night and when he called her for the sixth time, she finally answered the phone.

He was boiling. "Where the hell were you?" he demanded. "I waited for you for nearly an hour."

"What do you care," she answered. "Maybe I didn't feel like letting you ditch me over dinner, so I ditched you first." There was a long silence on the other end, then Bob started to laugh.

"You dope," he chortled. "I wasn't going to break up with you; I was going to ask you to go to Hawaii!"

Lucky for Sylvia, Bob had a sense of humor and knew her well enough to follow up with her.

The Synergy Antidote: When you find yourself assuming the worst, stop immediately and replace the negative picture in your mind with something positive. When your boss says, "Step into my office," set aside "Oh, now what did I do?" and think, "I'll bet she noticed what a great job I did on the XYZ project." This is right thinking.

Powerlessness

This particular thought pattern is insidious; we first encounter a lack of power when we are children and are subjected to the feeling that authority figures hold all the control in their hands. As adults, the daily news reinforces our helpless feelings. And in some cultures power comes from the top down. When we get into the habit of thinking we have no power, we surrender our creativity and authenticity and open the door to hopelessness and even depression. Individuals who are secure with their personal power are the best team players and are unafraid to contribute and share ideas.

The Synergy Antidote: Start developing your ability to be more assertive. This might mean pursuing a cause, donating your time to something you care about such as the environment or community service. It might mean helping animals or other people. When you take action, and you are contributing to something that has great meaning to you, it's easier to find the power to express yourself confidently. As you learn and discover your voice, you can start putting your positive energy into a team project–making a difference for yourself, your team, and your company.

Roger Was the King of Powerlessness

Roger believed that he had no power to affect his life and was directed by others in virtually everything: Relationships, getting a decent job, working out, anything that would better his life. Until, one day, he rescued a kitten from some boys who were tormenting it. He took the little thing home, fed it with an eyedropper and a tiny spoon, and made an appointment at the vet. He named his cat Ferdinand and watched the scrawny kitten grow into a plump, self-satisfied cat.

For his part, Ferdinand sat on Roger's lap, demanded attention at sunrise, and hung around the house doing cute feline things. Roger, seeing the difference he'd made in Ferdie's life, started volunteering as a placement coordinator at an animal shelter and found that he wasn't powerless at all. He found reserves of determination he'd never known he possessed. A year later, he received an award from the shelter for placing more animals than anyone before him. At work he began to offer suggestions to solve certain problems and was called upon regularly to be part of a continuous improvement team.

Secure people make the best team players!

Judgment

Especially in the realm of business, and the highly educated, judging others seems a given, even entertainment, but can quickly become a counter productive nasty habit, guaranteed to make people feel resentful and less cooperative. Of course, a business team needs to set standards of performance and should hold all team members responsible and accountable for their individual results. Measurement of performance is one of the keys to ongoing success. Individual improvement flourishes in a motivational environment of challenge, trust, respect, recognition, and possibility. It's easier to judge than it is to coach. Don't use one standard to measure everyone on the team; that's dangerous and can lead to group think.

The Synergy Antidote: Focus on results and recognize the value of assisting team players who may need improvement. Stop any judgmental thoughts as soon as they happen. Become a coach and work with the team player to turn a weakness into a strength. Be like Melanie in *Gone With the Wind,* who when told Scarlett was chasing all the men at the party (as well as Melanie's fiancé, Ashley), said something like, "Nonsense! She's just high-spirited, that's all!"

Seek the greatness in yourself, others, and life!

Paul, the Lonely Know-It-All

Paul has an opinion on everything, and he's never fazed by new situations. His wife and kids, who know him best, know that his snap judgements also tend to be long-lasting prejudices. Some years ago, his older son, who attended college in a nearby town, arranged to bring his girlfriend to dinner to "meet the family." They had been dating for six months and he was serious about the girl. But right after the introductions were made, his father mouthed off.

"So," he boomed, "Dan tells me you're going to be a psychologist! What's the matter, couldn't get into med school?"

Dan married his girlfriend a few years later, and Paul doesn't understand why they only bring his grandchildren by on Christmas. He says his daughter-in-law is "standoffish." Since he retired, he notices more and more that he doesn't really have friends, and it's hard to strike up conversations with strangers. His wife doesn't listen to him anymore; she just nods and says, "Okay, Honey."

As for his sons, the "smart one" says he's too busy with work, and the "crybaby" has avoided his harsh criticisms since childhood. It hurts Paul's feelings that his sons don't like to be with him, but he doesn't know what to do about it. Paul has no awareness of how he affects others and has little awareness of the social impact of his competitive demeanor. He is insecure and unaware and will die a lonely man unless he recognizes that he needs to change his behavior.

Competition

Competition is the essence of the capitalistic society, and American children are taught to compete as a major part of their education. But competing sometimes means losing and feeling on trial, which goes with the territory. True competition begins within your own efforts to improve yourself. Incorrect competitiveness drives people away. It is difficult to be around someone who always wants to be the best at everything–the best in every crowd, the smartest person in the room.

<u>The Synergy Antidote:</u> Remember how you felt the last time you lost at something, anything? You probably felt stupid, embarrassed, like a loser. Now, realize that when you insist on making everything a competition, you create resentment in others. Avoid competitive interactions and catch yourself when you try to top someone conversationally or socially. Practice by backing away from needing to win and listen. Respond appropriately within the confines of the event or situation, be gracious. Finally, practice cooperative interactive hobbies such as dancing with a partner. Working with someone towards a common goal is the best way to understand the value of cooperation.

Richard, the Competitor

Richard used to be an extremely competitive guy, so competitive that he had lost important friendships over friendly games of poker. At work he was known as cutthroat and merciless to anyone who stood between him and the Vice Presidency. His attitude backfired when he was passed over because, as the President told him, "No one trusts you enough to work for you." That changed Richard's life. Suddenly he was faced with the realization that he couldn't be the best, because when it came to teamwork and cooperation, he was the absolute worst. He set about changing his ways.

He started by letting his 8-year-old son beat him at chess, something he'd never allowed to happen, reasoning that he didn't want to pamper the kid. When he saw the glow in his son's eyes, he realized what he'd been missing, and the two discussed the entire game with the passion of champions.

Next, with the help of a good counselor, Richard started modifying his behavior at work. He learned to stop interrupting people at meetings; and he joined the company volleyball league, even though he was awful at volleyball. He learned to be a gracious loser. He also started practicing supporting his coworkers when they had great ideas or successful strategies. Along the way, people started trusting him and he discovered for the first time what it meant to work in a happy environment. Richard's life became more pleasant, and he was easier to get along with, which made his wife happy, too. Today, Richard laughs about it. "When I stopped playing by my old dog-eat-dog rules, I won the game!"

Black and White Thinking

It's easy to fall into black and white thinking, because all the rules are established; there's no need to grapple with the nuances of decision-making. That is an extremely seductive place to be– wouldn't we all love the simplicity of knowing what's right at all times? But this sort of thought leaves no room for flexibility, for new situations, or for other people who may have their own take on reality. Reality isn't easy, and one of the responsibilities of being human is that of being able to change when the situation demands it.

The Synergy Antidote: Experiment with change! Shake things up a bit by having dessert first, by wearing mismatched socks, by varying your routine. Ask yourself, "What happens if I don't do my laundry on Friday? What if I decide to do it Wednesday instead?" or, "What if I do let my kid stay up an extra half-hour instead of rushing her into bed right after I've done the dinner dishes?" By making small changes, you open yourself up to the possibility of big changes. Like any muscle, your mental flexibility may need slow stretching, with gradually-increasing exercise to accomplish greater feats.

Mind-Reading

We all attempt mind-reading once in awhile, and some of us are better at it than others. People from abusive homes are particularly good at discerning the mood of a room or an individual, as mind-reading can be a highly effective safety tool for someone who may need to escape a potentially volatile situation. However, the habit of mind-reading can be stressful and harmful, as we imagine the worst of someone else's thoughts and react to what we expect rather than what we may actually encounter. Mind-reading rarely discerns the positive, and is another form of expecting the worst.

The Synergy Antidote: Like negative thinking, mind-reading is usually projecting a negative outcome. Check your perceptions against reality by asking people you trust to confirm or disconfirm your ideas. For example, if a friend seems distant and you aren't sure why, don't automatically assume it's because of something you did. Ask her, "Are you mad at me?" and listen carefully to her answer. If the answer is, "No, but I had a fight with my kid today, and the dog peed on the carpet, and I'm really tired," you can relax: It's not you! When you find yourself ruminating about what another person may think, tell yourself firmly to stop. Turn your attention to something else. Do it again and again, and your habit will change.

When Things Go Wrong-You Can't Shake Hands with a Fist

Conflict is unavoidable, but choice is optional and right thinking and the right attitude will make all the difference. Whether you see a conflict as an occasional challenge or a terrifying threat to your very being, recognize that you have the capability to choose how you will respond. The most prudent and right response is to think as objectively as possible. Be honest with yourself when assessing what the real problem might be. Recognize that sometimes an outburst stands in for something bigger and more threatening to talk about. Calmly ask questions to open up the way to the real issue. Once you know what the real problem is, you can think about the right synergy antidote.

Nobody wants to talk about the elephant in the middle of the room.

This is an important time to use your logic and your emotions in problem-solving. Pay attention to your feelings expressly for the purpose of avoiding more conflict generated by hurt feelings or wounded egos. In an emotionally-charged situation, the first temptation is to look for competitive solutions or to go off on defensive tangents about who is right. Arguing about who is right only delays achieving a solution. What's important is not who is right, but what is right.

When we try to resolve conflict by way of power struggles, we are using win-lose thinking, which is exactly the opposite of synergistic thinking. Win-lose thinking causes wars. Wars may start because of something as small and manageable as a trade agreement. Don't let disagreements escalate to the point of major losses for all. It's primitive and uncivilized, and destroys the past, present, and future. There is a better way: the triple-win solution, which requires an advanced way of right thinking about work, life, and relationships. Triple win focuses on turning any situation into success. It explores the possibility of everyone gaining or achieving satisfaction, no matter what the circumstances are. Triple-win thinking and practice makes for true conflict resolution. Triple-win takes more thought, work, and creativity at the outset, but in the end the energy, productivity, and financial savings are huge.

Using triple-win in conflict resolution, the focus cannot be on blame or judgement. Choosing the correct focus invites proactive responses. Find and focus on the positive connections and agreements between you and the other person, not on the areas where you might have a difference. Don't argue; negotiate and stay calm. Nobody ever won an argument with a customer or the boss. Nobody has ever won the hearts and minds of others by trying to always outsmart them. Leave misplaced egos out of conflict situations. Be a bridge builder. Humor is a great connector, but do not make light of a person's opinion or point of view. Have a keen sense of awareness of body language and actively listen to the meaning behind the words. Understand that people often have difficulty describing what they mean. Out of respect for yourself, others, and for resolution, take time and care when engaged in conflict. Speak respectfully, keep your dignity and the dignity of others intact, and phrase things as carefully but as candidly as you can. If you feel things are worsening, or you just can't seem to get through, consider taking a break, and return when things (and people) are calmer. There is a lot to be said for "counting to ten."

It takes character and a sense of inner security to forgive and let go. Letting go, in the context of synergizing, is knowing that emotions can sometimes override our better judgements. Letting go and moving on must be the ultimate goal, even when our egos want to hold on to the 3.R's. This is tough, especially when we've been deeply hurt. We may have to practice letting go of the situation first and then learn to forgive. Most people have learned the opposite, to attack, to hate, and get even.

The moment we choose to let go, our thoughts, feelings body language and words will change. Forgiveness and, to a lesser degree, acceptance always project positive energy.

Project Positive Energy

Communication is not only about the words we use. Words can be misconstrued, not understood, and not heard. Words travel on positive or negative energy. A large part of communication is about having the right mental attitude and projecting positive energy.

The receiver of a message does not only hear words, but feels the energy that the words are traveling on and analyses information based on visual cues and body language. Behavior and body language are reflections of our thoughts and feelings. Eye movements, hand movements, body postures and expressions all form a visual and sensory perception of what we are saying.

"Who you are speaks so loudly, I can't hear what you're saying."

-Ralph Waldo Emerson

Steps to Resolving Conflict

The first step is to be maintain objectivity–don't get caught in the negative Synergy vortex. The focus should always be: "What is the real problem?"

The second step is to avoid ego and defensive comparisons such as, who is right. Who is right, will only delay achieving a solution. It's not who is right, but what is the right thing to do. Power struggles are not constructive and are based on win-lose interacting. Solving conflict is important in the achievement of an ongoing triple-win relationship.

The third step should be resolution, not blame and judgement. The point is to focus attention in the right place. In this way, we invite objectivity, reduce defensiveness, and focus on solutions.

It's you and me against the problem; not you and me against each other.

The fourth step is to gather the facts, but always from the position of "what-can-be-learned?" The truth can never be partial, and partiality can never be the complete truth.

The fifth step is to work as a team and focus on positive connections between you and the other person, not on the areas of difference. Agree with something: Even the smallest agreement can reduce conflict and begin the process of building Synergy.

Focus on looking past someone's quirks of nature so as to avoid feelings of resistance that may negatively influence a positive outcome,.

"Nobody can make you angry
without your permission."

-Eleanor Roosevelt

The sixth step is to reduce tension. When tension rises, ears close. If you have ever seen two people in an argument, screaming at one another, you would have noticed that it is a one-way power struggle where no one wins and everyone loses. If the conflict has reached such a point that communication is difficult, slow down and take it one situation at a time.

The seventh step is to seek Present Moment Synergy in communication as a fuel for teamwork. Focus on looking for solutions, new ideas, and ways to solve problems. Try to discover completely new and even better ways to work together.

Often, arrogant, obnoxious behavior can elicit a reactive response. It takes objectivity and strength to remain calm. Many interpersonal conflicts are created through reactive behavior. It is so easy to get hooked into someone's negativity. Negative energy is contagious.

Imagine arriving at work and you notice a team member is frustrated and angry about something.

Reactively, you say, "What's the problem?"

"Well, someone around here messed up the order and the boss just jumped on me. That's the problem."

You know that he was inferring that you messed up the order.

"Well, it wasn't me that screwed up."

"Well, somebody did. There must be an invisible man around here!"

"You know what, John? Take a hike."

"You take a hike! It's you that messed up!"

"You know what: You're a jerk, and I don't want to work with you."

If this scene sounds familiar, then you will know that reactive behavior can be a team work destroyer.

Now, imagine the same scene again. This time, you arrive at work and you notice your team member is angry. You immediately think Synergy and say:

"Is there something I can help you with?"

"Somebody has messed up here."

"Well, that may have been me, I apologize if it was. Let's fix it first and then we can find out what went wrong, okay?"

"Okay, let's do that!"

"Great. What's the most urgent thing to do?"

"You better call the customer and let them know that the order will need to be reshipped."

"Great! I'll do that right away."

Remember, it takes two to play a negative reactive game. Don't get caught in a negative trap. Stay objective and focused on helping the situation improve. It's you and me against the problem.

Most anger and reactiveness stem from work overload, staff shortage, a lack of attention, lack of recognition, or unresolved historic baggage. Historic baggage can revive many old negative feelings. This means that an individual's reasoning may not be in the present moment, and may not be rational and logical.

The best way to be rational is to stay in the present moment and have a heightened sense of awareness. The danger is allowing ourselves to get caught up in old ways of handling conflict.

We can all travel back to the past and hook old childish or parental behaviors and display them during a current conflict. Childish reactions from the past may be whining, complaining, sulking, temper tantrums, and so on. Past parental behaviors may be bossiness, judging, criticizing, advising, and generally being too controlling. The key is to recognize and become aware of your own historic behaviors, set them aside, and be flexible with others who are having play backs from way back.

You do this by engaging in a present-moment interactive flow of communication, actively listening, looping back, and practicing the art of being right here right now–giving your entire attention to resolving the problem.

Ask meaningful questions and wait for logical responses; and, if you need to, write things down. In this way, you respond efficiently and effectively which, in turn, will help to change feelings and behaviors and keep you in the here and now. It takes practice to ramp up your awareness, have a great attitude, and actively be a great team player.

If we believe in Synergy, if we believe in peace, if we believe that our minds and bodies are healthier by reducing tension and stress, then we work toward reconciling our differences and moving on with growing our contributions to the shared destiny.

Micro-Managers, Terrorist Bosses, and Others

When you have a boss who believes in teamwork and believes that each person must be given the right tools and the right climate to succeed, the potential for extraordinary results is accelerated. Less than ideal is a micro-managing boss who doesn't believe that people will work without being closely attended. Micro-managers who mean well can usually be reasoned with. Horrific is the terrorist boss who probably knows you could do the work better without fear but who takes pleasure in ridiculing team players and creating fear to satisfy his insecure control needs. Terrorist bosses, who will not be reasoned with, deserve to be left alone with their weird enjoyments while you find someone better with whom to work. If your capacity for Synergy is being interfered with, it's up to you to find a way to change the situation.

Sometimes you can do everything right, but if the people you work with are playing with hidden agendas, everyone will lose. Ideally, it should be possible to tell at an interview if you're headed into a bad place, but interviews are like first dates: It's difficult to really know what you're getting before you're already committed. If the people you work with aren't playing by the standard rules of respect and courtesy, the wise thing is to get out as soon as possible and find a civilized organization with good leadership. Avoid toxicity and all forms of narcissism.

Narcissist's have it easy.

Interpersonal Communication Is the Soul Food of Synergy

Like much success in life, Synergy happens by choosing to communicate. We can influence and encourage the growth of Synergy by being attentive to the needs of the team. Encouraging Synergy in your work life requires a certain amount of self-management and enough flexibility to meet your needs and the needs of the team. The perfect environment to allow your creativity and competency to flourish is an environment that is high on communication and free of fear.

Communication is the soul food of personal relationships, families, businesses, cities, and nations.

The goal of Synergy is the compounded value achieved from working together toward a shared destiny. The idea is that through excellent communication, we can reach out and expand the capability of each team member, thus enhancing the potential for greater workmanship and job enrichment.

Two or more minds connected can create a powerful opportunity to trust, understand and accept other points of view.

Synergy is all about connecting and communicating. If your customer wins, they are happy. If your company wins, everyone within it is happy; if your industry wins, it manifests growth; and, if you win, your family wins, your city wins, and ultimately the nation wins. Synergy builds customer loyalty, company profitability, and employment security.

When we treat each other with dignity, respect, and efficiency, we create a culture of cooperative high-performance, which ripples out to the customer!

Synergy Behavior Matrix

*"Oh, would some power the gift give
us, to see ourselves as others see us."*

-Robert Burns

In our Synergy Team Power seminars, we coach teams on how to implement the 5 success habits as laid out in this book along with the four interpersonal communication styles; Director, Evaluator, Harmonizer, and Initiator.

Evaluators	Low	Harmonizers
Calm, Non-Contentious, Detailed, Gathers Facts Before Deciding		Loyal, Friendly, Supportive, Easy Going, Empathetic
When Communicating: Take Your Time, Give Lots of Info, Be Specific and Encourage Opinions		**When Communicating:** Create Relationships, Be Friendly, Talk People Not Things

Low	Expression	Dominance	Expression	High

Directors	High	Initiators
Dominant, Determined, Very Decisive and Challenging		Enthusiastic, Excitable, Creative, Spontaneous, Argumentative, Manipulative
When Communicating: Be Direct, To the Point, Be Efficient, Be Businesslike		**When Communicating:** Be Fun, Be Quick, Show Confidence, Offer Opportunity

The Director is an individual who likes to direct, control, organize, set goals, and is very task oriented.

The Evaluator is an individual who likes to analyze, nitpick, work things out, weigh things up, and think things over.

The Harmonizer is a very social, outgoing, friendly, and gregarious individual, who is low on assertiveness.

The Initiator is an outgoing, fun, lively, and assertive individual.

Different styles approach problems differently, communicate differently, and interpret things in unique ways. High-performance teams require different styles and different perspectives, and bring unique special talents to the table–the perfect way to a synergized workplace! But differences in styles also cause conflict and, as a good team player, you want to be prepared to minimize conflict while making the most of everything your team has to contribute.

In order to build better teams we need to know how to get on with all styles. Focusing on Synergy and the strengths of others helps smooth out the rough spots and focus on the goal, e.g., if you happen to be an Evaluator, you need to know how to deal with an Initiator, which is your opposite style. If you don't, that person's going to irritate you all day long. If you are a Director, you need to know how to get along with Harmonizers, and so on. The key is to focus on all interpersonal communication styles and their contribution to the team goals. In this way, you build a sense of belonging and team synergy.

Synergy in communication happens when two people actively work on first understanding each other's point of view.

Choosing to build a high-performance team means you have to love the idea of winning through people. It requires learning how to lead, coach, nurture, and discipline a team of super-achievers focused on a shared destiny. The results will astonish you!

Why Don't They Just Synergize?

Frank, V.P. of Corporate Communications

"Another meeting, thought Frank. Nothing will be accomplished beyond irritation and conflict. I'm not going to contribute anything, that's the easiest way to get it over with. I can't stand Ellen; she is so impatient and pushy. I'm sure she thinks that she should be the boss. Imagine working for her; communication would be one way: Her way or the highway. I'm sure quite a few people would resign under her leadership. She could certainly lighten up. Anyway, today I'll try and be proactive and ignore her personal remarks. I like Mark and Mary. Mary is pretty outgoing, maybe a little too much, but I like her. Mark makes good suggestions in the meeting. I just wish he would talk a little more."

Mary, V.P. of Regional Sales

"Great, I'm looking forward to this meeting. I have quite a few things I want to change. I've got to get Mark to see the bigger picture. He is so damn analytical, I wish he wouldn't slow down everything by analyzing every word I say and examining every detail. It drives me crazy! Ellen is okay, but she's angry about something. I wish I knew what it was. She's so serious. Her and Mark–do they ever party! Anyway, I like Frank, he's easygoing, and he kind of goes along with most of what I ask him to do. I like that! I'm going to try and get him on my side to get the rest of them to go along with my suggestions."

Ellen, V.P. of Production

"What a waste of time! I have so much to do and now I have to attend another meeting. How can any of these people help with anything at all, especially Frank? All he wants to do is socialize and ask everyone how they feel. What do they do in communications anyway?–talk, talk, talk–when they should be doing something constructive. We have so many goals we have to achieve and work to do that I don't want to waste my time with the Franks, Marks, and Marys of this world. I'm an action person. I'm going to take over the meeting, control it, set some goals, and get out and do some important work–which is not in this meeting."

Mark, V.P. of Finance

"I wonder if this meeting will be as generalized as all the rest. We never seem to get into the details of things. The one thing I cannot stand, is how Mary sprouts one opinion after another without anything to back it up. I just know it will work, she says and that drives me bananas. How can anyone just know without facts? I have an agenda of what needs to be covered and copies for everyone, and that should help a lot. If we just go through it step-by-step, it will help the group become more systematic. It should keep Ellen from bullying Frank again and Mary from going off on a tangent. I'll see how this works and ask everyone how they like the agenda and if they do, we can use it every time. Better get into the meeting, only five minutes to spare."

These are four members of a company on their way to a monthly meeting. Very little is ever accomplished beyond irritation and interpersonal conflict.

Frank rarely contributes anymore. He tries to reduce conflict by making small talk and silly jokes. He compliments people and tries to make everyone feel good–even Ellen who dislikes it and shows it by making belittling remarks. Frank never confronts her.

Mary is great at sales. She is lively, opinionated, loves her job, and her numbers reflect her ability. She wants the monthly meeting to work and always has a flow of great ideas, which she loves to share.

Ellen is irritated by the lack of direction and mostly by Frank. This meeting is a waste of time, so she wants to get it over with as soon as possible. She demonstrates her impatience by taking charge and by rushing through every point.

Mark is super analytical and believes everyone should be that way. He can't understand why the group is so unstructured. He stays away from the conflict between Ellen and Frank because, to him, it is not sensible or logical.

The negative attitudes and an unwillingness to work together in the group discussed above has created a meeting experience full of tension and withdrawal, which has flowed over from one meeting to the next. The result is a growing prejudice that's unproductive and a waste of time and money. The pillars of Synergy are: Trust, right mental attitude, be the first-giver, and make it fun. When all of these are practiced, the result is the multiplying power of Synergy. This team must focus on the strengths that each person can contribute and lead to a feeling of mutual respect and trust. Without trust and respect, it is difficult to build Synergy. With greater awareness and willing present-moment communication, they can deliberately shift the interpersonal negativity that's making their meeting so unproductive.

As a general rule, meetings are held to solve problems, make decisions, and bring everyone onto the same page! The goal of Synergy is the compounded value achieved from working together. Everyone is rewarded. The foundation of Synergy is trust and the essence is experience!

The key is to set aside prejudice and focus on understanding how to work together rather than against each other. Focusing on a common goal and redirecting energy toward a positive outcome helps to build a better appreciation of the abilities and talents of our teammates. Shared success has a way of defusing anger and tension. One of the most successful ways to improve Synergy is to accommodate the style of the person with whom we are dealing. We can choose to shift from needing to be heard to listening to the needs of our coworkers. Practicing social and emotional intelligence plays an important role in building collaboration. The Synergy Behavior Matrix demonstrates how to apply interpersonal flexibility by consciously trying to give other behavior styles what they need. By doing so, individuals in teams can vastly elevate interpersonal connection and collaboration. This – like all communication – can be learned and improved by practicing daily.

In the case study above, Frank, who is a Harmonizer, could easily shift his thinking to Synergy–rather than be put off by Ellen. If he moved away from his Harmonizer world and stepped over into the Director's world, he would be able to get to the point quicker, and not over-socialize or become defensive.

Ellen, who is a Director, could synergize by recognizing that Frank has great strengths, particularly his interpersonal and people skills, and that most people warm to Harmonizers. When dealing with Frank, she should appeal to him as a person rather than as a task.

Mary, who is an Initiator, could recognize that Mark is more analytical than he is creative, and she could relate more to his strength: his logic. If she presented her ideas in a logical, preferably written format, Mark would suddenly become quite agreeable.

Mark, an Evaluator, could shift his rigidness and listen more carefully to Mary, and maybe make his own notes, which would not only please Mary but Mark may find there is a great merit in Mary's ideas.

Although no one in the meeting is especially comfortable with the process, far and away the unhappiest person in the room is Ellen. Ellen is in an unhappy spot because she has strong leadership tendencies, but has found herself in a position where she is not able to exercise them. Ideally, someone in upper management will pick up on Ellen's organizational capacity and drive and start using them by giving her more responsibility.

An important component of working well as a team is being aware that the differences between people make up a team's unique strength. Taking different talents into account is a smart way of allocating work. For example, we need two people to head up the committee for the Christmas party. Pairing up Frank and Mary wouldn't be very effective because their interactions tend to be more playful than planful. However, pairing Mary with Mark might work out fine, since Mary can publicize the event, talk to people about food and gifts, and add a fun touch, while Mark can create a time-line, handle the budget, and arrange to rent the space. Their strengths are complementary.

At every level of an organization, it's possible to build Synergy by using the unique talents of all team members and by being open to different ideas. This creates an inspirational atmosphere where respectful communication is the norm.

The single constant to success
is Synergy!

The Guru and the Abuse

It is said that on an occasion when the Guru was teaching a group of people, he found himself on the receiving end of a fierce outburst of abuse from a bystander, who was for some reason very angry.

The Guru listened patiently while the stranger vented his rage, and then the Guru said to the group and to the stranger, "If someone gives a gift to another person, who then chooses to decline it, tell me, who would then own the gift? The giver or the person who refuses to accept the gift?"

"The giver," said the group after a little thought. "Any fool can see that," added the angry stranger.

"Then it follows, does it not," said the Guru, "whenever a person tries to abuse us, or to unload their anger on us, we can each choose to decline or to accept the abuse; whether to make it ours or not. By our personal response to the abuse from another, we can choose who owns and keeps the bad feelings."

-Author Unknown

Having no awareness is like being given an open book exam and forgetting to bring the book!

Which of these are you?

Some members keep a group so strong,

while others join just to belong.

Some dig right in; serve with pride;

Some go along just for the ride.

Some volunteer to do their share,

While some lie back and just don't care.

Some do their best, some help, some make;

Some do nothing, only take.

Some greet new members with a smile,

And make their coming so worthwhile,

While some go on their merry way,

No greeting or kind word to say.

Which one are you?

Some help the group to grow and grow,

When asked to help, they don't say 'No'.

Some drag, some pull, some don't, some do;

Consider, which of these are you?

-Author Unknown

20 Ways to Be a Synergist

1. Build communication bridges and break down silos and walls of conflict.

2. Focus on strengths, contributions and talents of every team player.

3. Believe that "teamwork is the secret."

4. Wear the right face when communicating with team players.

5. Adjust your style to meet team players' and customers' styles.

6. Think triple-win; your customer wins, your company wins, and you win . . . in that order.

7. Under-promise and over-deliver.

8. Be respectful, courteous, and polite.

9. Send thank you notes and show genuine appreciation for a job well done.

10. When making decisions, think about all the consequences, people, and situations they may affect.

11. Be open, candid, and sincere but kind and tactful.

12. Don't dwell on past mistakes, focus on a shared destiny.

13. Make yourself easier to work with-project positive energy.

14. Do not gossip or talk about another team player. If you have a problem, work it out and move on.

15. Leave your ego at the door.

16. Avoid passive-aggressive behavior. Enforce the "no pouting" rule.

17. Bring balance into your workplace by building relationship bridges and making work fun.

18. Always admit your mistakes and apologize when you're wrong.

19. Share knowledge and information, you can never lose it by giving it away.

20. You cannot whistle a symphony on your own. Synergy compounds if you work at it.

In Conclusion

Synergy Team Power is the foundation of the Synergy people centered change formula and has proven to be successful in many companies and industries worldwide. When an organization comes together and is united behind a common set of goals and core values, the potential for extraordinary achievement is unlimited and without boundaries.

High-performance business teams are well structured, coached, nurtured, developed and disciplined. Discipline is the bedfellow of teamwork and improves the quality of workmanship across the board. Training, education, good systems and structure are fundamental to making your team world-class. The Synergy magic happens through the team's combined effort and commitment to practice a given set of core values.

Practicing core values and insisting that core values become a platform for decision making will teach employees how to build relationship trust, loyalty, commitment and respect. The environment, climate and culture all play a major role in marshaling the collective brain power and creative energy of your team. Therein lies the true source of power.

Selected Bibliography

Albion, Mark. Making a Life, Making a Living. New York: Warner Books, 2000.

Albrecht, Carl. At America's Service. New York: Warner Books, Inc., 1992.

Alexander, Chris. Creating Extraordinary Joy. Alameda: Hunter House, 2001.

_____. Synergizing Your Business. Lake Forest, CA: 1+1=3 Publishing, 2002.

_____. Joy in the Workplace. Lake Forest, CA: 1+1=3 Publishing, 2003.

_____. Synergy Strategic Planning. Lake Forest, CA: 1+1=3 Publishing, 2010.

Allen, James. As a Man Thinketh. Mount Vernon, NY: The Peter Pauper Press, date not listed.

Autry, James. Real Power. New York: River head Books, 1998.

Barker, Joel Arthur. Paradigms: The Business of Discovering the Future. New York, NY: HarperCollins Publishers, Inc., 1992.

Beatty, Jack. The World According to Peter Drucker. New York: The Free Press, 1998.

Beene, R. Timothy S., Paul F. Nunes, and Walter E. Shill. "The Chief Strategy Officer." Harvard Business Review, October 2007: 84-91.

Bennis, Warren. On Becoming a Leader. Reading, MA: Addison-Wesley Publishing Company, 1989.

Berne, Eric. Games People Play. New York: Grove Press, 1964.

Blanchard, Kenneth and Spencer Johnson. The One Minute Manager. New York: Berkley Books, 1982.

Blanchard, Ken and Sheldon Bowles. Gung Ho! New York: William Morrow and Company, Inc., 1998.

Blanchard, Ken, Jim Ballard, and Fred Finch. Customer Mania! New York: Simon & Schuster, Inc., 2004.

Bonstingl, John Jay. Schools of Quality. Thousand Oaks, CA: Corwin Press, Inc., 2001.

Borysenko, Joan and Miroslav. The Power of the Mind to Heal. Carlsbad, CA: Hay House, 1996.

Bossidy, Larry and Ram Charan. Execution. New York: Crown Business, 2002.

Bower, Joseph L. and Clark G. Gilbert. "How Managers' Everyday Decisions Create - or Destroy - Your Company's Strategy." Harvard Business Review, February 2007: 72-79.

Bruce, Anne and James S. Pepitone. Motivating Employees. Madison, WI. McGraw-Hill, 1999.

Buscaglia, Leo F. Living, Loving & Learning. New York: Ballantine Books, 1983.

Butler, Gillian and Tony Hope. Managing Your Mind. New York: Oxford University Press, 1995.

Byham, William C. Zapp! The Lighting of Empowerment. New York: Ballantine Books, 1988.

Capodagli, Bill and Lynn Jackson. The Disney Way. New York: McGraw-Hill, 1999.

Charan, Ram. Know-How. New York. Random House, Inc., 2007.

Christensen, Clayton M., Stephen P. Kaufman, and Willy C. Shih. "Innovation Killers: How Financial Tools Destroy Your Capacity to Do New Things." Harvard Business Review - Leadership & Strategy for the Twenty-first Century, January 2008: 98-105.

Collins, James C. and Jerry I. Porras. Built to Last. New York: HarperCollins Publishers Inc., 1994.

Collins, Jim. Good to Great. New York: HarperCollins Publishers Inc., 2001.

Covey, Stephen R. The 7 Habits of Highly Effective People. New York: Simon & Schuster, Inc., 1990.

_____. Principle-Centered Leadership. New York: Simon & Schuster, Inc., 1992.

Dell, Chip R. Managers as Mentors. San Francisco, CA: Berrett-Koehler Publishers, Inc., 1996.

DeLong, Thomas J., John J. Gabarro, and Robert J. Lees. "Why Mentoring Matters in a Hypercompetitive World." Harvard Business Review - Leadership & Strategy for the Twenty-first Century, January 2008: 115-121.

Denove, Chris and James D. Power IV. Satisfaction. New York: Penguin Group, 2006.

De Pree, Max. Leadership Jazz. New York: Dell Publishing, 1993.

DeVos, Rich. Compassionate Capitalism. New York: Penguin Group, 1994.

Dodd, Dominic and Ken Favaro. "Managing the Right Tension." Harvard Business Review, December 2006: 62-74.

Dotlich, David L. and Peter C. Cairo. Action Coaching. San Francisco, CA: Jossey-Bass Publishers, 1999.

Drucker, Peter F. The New Realities. New York: Harper and Row Publishers, 1989.

_____. The Effective Executive. New York: Harper and Row Publishers, 1996.

_____. Management Challenges for the Twenty First Century. New York: HarperCollins Publishers Inc., 1999.

Elkin, Allen. Stress Management for Dummies. Foster City, CA: IDG Books Worldwide, Inc., 1999.

Freiberg, Kevin and Jackie. Nuts! Southwest Airlines' Crazy Recipe for Business and Personal Success. Austin, TX: Bard Press, 1996.

Fuller, R. Buckminster. Synergetics: Explorations in the Geometry of Thinking. New York: MacMillan Publishers, 1975.

Gallo, Fred P. Energy Psychology. Boca Raton, FL: CRC Press, 1999.

Gardner, Howard. "The Ethical Mind." Harvard Business Review, March 2007: 51-56.

Gerber, Michael. The E-Myth Manager. New York: HarperCollins Publishers Inc., 1998.

Goffee, Rob and Gareth Jones. "Leading Clever People." Harvard Business Review, March 2007: 72-79.

Goleman, Daniel. Emotional Intelligence. New York: Bantam Books, 1995.

Goleman, Daniel, Richard Boyatzis, and Annie McKee. Primal Leadership: Learning to Lead with Emotional Intelligence. Boston, MA: Harvard Business School, 2002.

Greenleaf, Robert K. On Becoming a Servant Leader. Edited by Frick, Don M. and Spears, Larry C. San Francisco, CA: Jossey-Bass Publishers, 1996.

Greiner, Donna and Kinni, Theodore B. 1,001 Ways to Keep Customers Coming Back. Rocklin, CA: Prima Publishing, 1999.

Hammer, Kay. Workplace Warrior. New York: AMA Publications, 2000.

Handy, Charles. The Hungry Spirit. New York: Bantam Doubleday Dell Publishing Groups, Inc., 1998.

Hawkins, David R. Power vs. Force. Carlsbad, CA: Hay House, Inc., 2002.

Henricks, Mark. Grow Your Business. Irvine, CA: Entrepreneur Press, 2001.

Hill, Linda A. "Where Will We Find Tomorrow's Leaders?" Harvard Business Review - Leadership & Strategy for the Twenty-first Century, January 2008: 123-129.

Hill, Napoleon. Think and Grow Rich. North Hollywood, CA: Wilshire Book Company, 1966.

_____. Law of Success. Chicago, IL: Success Unlimited, Inc., 1979.

Hogan, Eve Eschner, with Steven Hogan. Intellectual Foreplay. Alameda, CA: Hunter House, 2000.

Holmes, Ernest. The Science of Mind. New York: Dodd, Mead, and Company, 1938.

Jampolsky, Gerald. Love is Letting Go of Fear. Berkeley, CA: Celestial Arts, 1979.

John Paul II, His Holiness. Crossing the Threshold of Hope. New York: Random House, 1994.

Kanter, Rosabeth Moss. "Transforming Giants." Harvard Business Review - Leadership & Strategy for the Twenty-first Century, January 2008: 43-52.

Kaplan, Robert S. and David P. Norton. "Mastering the Management System." Harvard Business Review - Leadership & Strategy for the Twenty-first Century, January 2008: 62-77.

Katzenbach, Jon R. and Douglas K. Smith. The Wisdom of Teams. New York: Harvard Business School Press, 1993.

Kouzes, James M. and Barry Z. Posner. The Leadership Challenge. San Francisco, CA: Jossey-Bass Publishers, 1995.

Krieger, Robert J. and Louis Patler. If it ain't broke...Break it! New York: Warner Books, Inc., 1991.

Leadership . . . with a Human Touch. Jan 18, 1994; May 10, 1994; May 9, 1995; June 6, 1995. Economics Press, Inc., Fairfield, NJ.

Lencioni, Patrick. The Five Dysfunctions of a Team, San Francisco, CA: Jossey-Bass Publishers, 2002.

Loehr, Jim and Tony Schwartz. The Power of Full Engagement. New York: Free Press, 2003.

Logan, Dave, John King, and Halee Fischer-Wright. Tribal Leadership. New York: HarperCollins Publishers Inc., 2008.

Lindbergh, Anne Morrow. Gifts from the Sea. New York: Pantheon Book, Inc., 1955.

Maltz, Maxwell. Psycho-Cybernetics. Hollywood, CA: Wilshire Book Company, 1965.

Mandino, Og. The Greatest Salesman in the World. New York: Bantam Books, 1968.

_____. The Greatest Miracle in the World. New York: Bantam Books, 1975.

_____. The Greatest Salesman in the World, Part II, New York: Bantam Books, 1988.

Mann, Nancy R. The Keys to Excellence. The Deming Philosophy. London, England: Mercury Books, 1989.

Marriott, J.W. Jr. and Kathi Ann Brown. The Spirit to Serve. New York: HarperCollins Publishers, Inc., 1997.

Martin, Roger. "How Successful Leaders Think." Harvard Business Review, June 2007: 60-67.

McBride, Linda. The Mass Market Woman. Eagle River, Alaska: Crowded Hour Press, 1999.

McWilliams, John-Roger and Peter McWilliams. Life 101: You Can't Afford the Luxury of a Negative Thought. Los Angeles, CA: Prelude Press, 1988.

_____. Life 101. Los Angeles, CA: Prelude Press, 1991.

Medina, John J. "The Science of Thinking Smarter." Harvard Business Review, May 2008: 51-54.

Montgomery, Cynthia A. "Putting Leadership Back into Strategy." Harvard Business Review - Leadership & Strategy for the Twenty-first Century, January 2008: 54-60.

Montrose, Philip. Getting through to Your Emotions with EFT. Sacramento, CA: Holistic Communications, 2000.

Moore, Thomas. Original Self. New York: HarperCollins Publishers Inc., 1981.

Neidert, David. Four Seasons of Leadership. Provo, UT: Executive Excellence Publishing, 1999.

Nerburn, Kent and Louise Mengelkoch. Native American Wisdom. San Rafael, CA: New World Library, 1991.

Nerburn, Kent. The Soul of an Indian. San Rafael, CA: New World Library, 1993.

Novak, Philip. The World's Wisdom. Edison, NJ: Castle Books, 1996.

Ornish, Dean. Love and Survival: The Scientific Basis for the Healing Power of Intimacy. New York: HarperCollins Publishers Inc., 1998.

Palmer, Parker J. Active Life. San Francisco, CA: Jossey-Bass Publishers, 1990.

_____. Let your Life Speak. San Francisco, CA: Jossey-Bass Publishers, 2000.

Pearsall, Paul. The Pleasure Prescription. Alameda, CA: Hunter House, 1998.

Peck, M. Scott. The Road Less Traveled. New York: Simon & Schuster, Inc., 1978.

Pert, Candace and Deepak Chopra. Molecules of Emotion. New York: Scribner, 1997.

Peters, Thomas J. and Robert H. Waterman, Jr. In Search of Excellence. New York: Warner Books, 1982.

_____. Thriving on Chaos. New York: Harper Perennial, 1987.

_____. Liberation Management. New York: Alfred A. Knopf, 1992.

Plunket, Warren R., Raymond F. Attner, and Gemmy S. Allen. Management: Meeting and Exceeding Customer Expectation, 8th Edition. Mason: Thompson South-Western, 2005.

Porter, Michael E. "The Five Competitive Forces That Shape Strategy." Harvard Business Review - Leadership & Strategy for the Twenty-first Century, January 2008: 78-93.

Robbins, Anthony. Awaken the Giant Within. New York: Summit Books, 1991.

Russell, Peter. The Brain Book. New York: Penguin Group, 1979.

Schein, Edgar H. Organizational Culture and Leadership. San Francisco, CA: Jossey-Bass, 2004.

Senge, Peter M. The Fifth Discipline. New York: DoubleDay, 1994.

Simon, David. Vital Energy. New York: Wiley, 2000.

Slone, Reuben E., John T. Meltzer, and J. Paul Dittman. "Are You the Weakest Link in Your Company's Supply Chain?" Harvard Business Review, September 2007: 116-127.

Spector, Robert and Patrick D. McCarthy. The Nordstrom's Way: The Inside Story of America's # 1 Customer Service Company. New York: John Wiley and Sons, Inc., 1995.

Spitzer, Robert J. The Spirit of Leadership. Provo, UT: Executive Excellence Publishing, 2000.

Stanley, Andy. Visioneering. Sisters, OR: Multnomah Publishers, Inc., 1999.

Star, Jonathan. Rumi. New York: Penguin Putnam Inc., 1997.

Staub, Robert E. II. The Acts of Courage. Provo, UT: Executive Excellence Publishing, 1999.

Stevenson, Howard H. "How to Change the World." Harvard Business Review - Leadership & Strategy for the Twenty-first Century, January 2008: 29-33.

Steward, Marjabelle Young and Marian Faux. Executive Etiquette in the New Workplace. New York: St. Martin's Press, 1994.

Thomas, R. David. Dave's Way. New York: Berkley Books, 1992.

Thompson, G. Liam. E-Business to Go. St. Louis, MO: Appollaso Publishing, 2001.

Thoreau, Henry David. Walden and Other Writings. New York: Barnes & Noble Books, 1993.

Tracy, Brian. The 100 Absolutely Unbreakable Laws of Business Success. San Francisco, CA: Berrett-Koehler Publishers, Inc., 2000.

_____. Advance Selling Strategies. New York: Simon & Schuster, Inc., 1995.

Trimble, Vance H. Sam Walton, Founder of Walmart. New York: Penguin Books, 1990. Ward, Andrew J. et al. "Improving the Performance of Top Management Teams." MIT Sloan Management Review, Spring 2007: 85-90.

Wasserstein, Bruce. "The HBR Interview: Giving Great Advice." Harvard Business Review - Leadership & Strategy for the Twenty-first Century, January 2008: 106-113.

Welch, Jack. Jack, Straight from the Gut. New York: Warner Books, Inc., 2001.

_____. Winning. New York: HarperCollins Publishers Inc., 2005.

Wheatley, Margaret J. and Myron Kellner-Rogers, A Simpler Way. San Francisco, CA: Berrett-Koehler, 1996.

Wolf, Fred Alan. Mind into Matter. Portsmouth, NH: Moment Point Press, 2001.

Ziff, Lazer. Ralph Waldo Emerson - Selected Essays. New York: Penguin Books, 1984.

Zingheim, Patricia K. and J.R. Schuster. Pay People Right. San Francisco, CA: Jossey-Bass Publishers, 2000.

Zukav, Gary. The Seat of the Soul. New York: Fireside, 1989.

Synergizing Your Business:

The 5 Essential Pieces for
High-Performance
A Series of Business Books

by Chris Alexander

The 5 Essential Pieces

2. Strategic Planning Retreats

3. Leadership Skills Workshops

1. TEAM POWER RETREAT

5. Customized Sales Workshops

4. Customer Care Workshops

Teamwork Divides the Task and Doubles the Success!

Synergizing Your Business

The 5 Essential Pieces for High-Performance

The Synergy Formula, 1+1=3, energizes the people in your business to effectively work as a high-performance team. We are experts at getting an entire organization to 'play from the same sheet of music.' Our formula improves communication, builds trust and empowers individuals with a sense of purpose. We motivate everyone into taking greater responsibility and accountability for their jobs. When employees have a say in the things that affect them, they willingly give their best efforts and produce more, reduce costs and ultimately "WOW" customers.

Synergy workshops and seminars build relationship trust and break through walls of negativity and resistance. This allows the essential pieces for collaboration between management and employees to strengthen. The essential pieces of collaboration are vision ownership, core values, teamwork, WOW factor goals and a clearly defined shared destiny. When the motivational puzzle snaps together a greater sense of belonging and a culture of emotional security is formed resulting in a strong foundation for high-performance teamwork.

A major benefit within the Synergy Formula is our experience and ability to instantly tap into and direct the human energy source of a business. We have proven in company after company and industry after industry that harnessing human potential and energy and directing it toward a shared destiny multiplies the potential for success. We know how to create unstoppable, unflappable and unshakable zones of inspiration and secure, highly profitable businesses.

We focus on building shared responsibility, strong relationships, shared values, shared goals and collective spiritual agreements, all sources of inspiration and energy. The outcome, the greatest competitive advantage a business can possess, a team of professionals committed to WOWing customers.

Essential Piece #1:
Synergy Team Power:

The 5 Success Habits of
High-Performance Business Teams

Synergy Team Power is the foundation of the Synergy Formula and has proven to be successful in many companies and industries worldwide. When an organization comes together and is united behind a common set of goals and core values, the potential for extraordinary achievement is unlimited and without boundaries.

High-performance business teams need structured, ongoing coaching, nurturing, development and discipline. Discipline is the bedfellow of teamwork and improves the quality of workmanship across the board. Training, education, good systems and structure are fundamental to making your team world-class. The Synergy magic happens through the team's combined effort and commitment to practice a given set of core values.

Practicing core values and insisting that core values become a platform for decision making will teach employees how to build relationship trust, loyalty, commitment and respect. The environment and climate plays a major role in marshaling the collective brain power and creative energy of your team. Therein lies the true source of power.

Essential Piece # 2:
Synergy Strategic Planning:

A Blueprint for Organizational Planning and Execution

A good strategic plan focuses on integrating people, systems and structure, and directing them toward a predetermined and worthwhile exciting vision, a clear set of believable and livable values and Transformational, Exciting, Authentic, Measurable goals. (TEAM Goals)

The Vision needs to be clear, exciting, challenging and believable. It needs to build a clear picture of what shared success looks like down the road.

The Values need to be virtuous, such as building relationship trust through personal and professional respect, delivering quality products and embracing service to one another and the customer.

The Goal should clearly focus on achieving the vision, increasing profitability, productivity and performance with specific measurable sub-goals.

"Real Wealth Is Knowing How to Direct Energy."

- Buckminster Fuller

Systems, Structure and Functions

A key ingredient for a strategic plan to work is to ensure that systems, job functions and structure support the vision, values and goals. Working as a high-performance team and Exceeding Customer Expectations can die very quickly if dictatorial leadership and outdated policies and procedures block positive energy. Of course all systems, structure and functions cannot be changed overnight—that's why the Synergy Formula supports the principle of continuous improvement. Thousands of small changes made over time will transform a low performing outfit into a world-class organization—of that there is no doubt.

Management Commitment

A steady, consistent commitment and guiding hand will be the final component of a successful strategic plan. That means, attending meetings, living the values, embracing the vision and being accountable and delivering on the goals. In that way a leadership magnetism takes hold and energy and effort become authentic and trustworthy. To put it simply: anyone would like to work for a purpose-driven, trustworthy leader who walks the talk.

What Gets Measured Gets Done.

Essential Piece # 3:
Synergy Leadership Skills:

The Art and Practice of Building and Leading a High-Performance Business Team

Synergy leaders are the motivators and communicators of the vision, values and goals, initiating communication and building relationship trust. It is their responsibility to coach, counsel and mentor individuals through the process of organizational change. They build high-performance teamwork through daily practical behavioral application. From the CEO to the frontline manager, the integrity of the entire business depends upon whether the executive team practices good leadership principles and become the examples and catalysts for positive change.

When the leadership team is on the same page, the rest of the organization falls more easily into alignment. Understanding how to practice an accepted strong set of leadership behavioral skills creates a greater sense of competency in an employee's mind, particularly if the core values are seen to be practiced and supported. An attitudinal and loyalty Synergy glue is then created between management and staff.

We have all worked for companies that are confused about their leadership style. Unity of direction, leadership and consistent role modeling are critical components for success. They demonstrate that we are truly dedicated to building a culture of integrity.

Essential Piece #4:
Synergy "WOW" Factor!:

How to Bring The "WOW!" Factor into Your Business and Earn Customer Loyalty for Life

The Synergy "WOW" Factor! begins with treating everyone you work with as your customer. It incorporates the Golden Rule, "Treat others as you would like to be treated." Therefore, customer service is a worthy business core value, as well as an important personal one. Employees tend to treat customers as they are treated by the company. Bad service and bad attitudes are merely reflections of the way people have become accustomed to treating one another.

Synergy works from the "inside out" and it's paramount that everyone in every department understands the principle of service. Service from the internal to the external drives the financial engine of a business. Good service increases revenue, lowers costs and reduces staff attrition. Everyone should be service minded and empowered to solve problems immediately and directly. The senior executives, managers, service representatives, sales people and receptionists need to be committed to service. Trust and loyalty are reinforced when all customers are taken care of in an effective, efficient and friendly manner.

Essential Piece # 5:
Synergy Sales Power:
The Art and Skill of Relationship Selling

Synergy Sales Power focuses on the importance of building long-term, quality relationships with customers. As a part of the Synergy process, Sales Power focuses on building a solid reputation of trust by assisting the customer in establishing his/her true needs and wants.

Synergy focuses on relationship selling and building customers for life. Relationships are formed between people before contracts are signed.

Customers will act on recommendations from sales people they trust. Relationship selling is based on understanding the customer's buying style and adapting to it; building low cost customer retention for the company and happy and loyal customers.

By Synergizing with your customer, you are able to build highly profitable, triple-win relationships!

"Overall, Chris Alexander helped me gain confidence in myself, in my work, and in my personal life. Every time I walked out of that room, I was inspired and motivated to do something. I think his workshop has helped a lot of people here at White Sands."

-Carla Pineda, Community Relations and
Sales Coordinator,
White Sands of La Jolla

Chris Alexander
M.A. (Org. Psych.)

Professional Speaker, Award-Winning Business-Building Strategist and Author

If you would like to hear the words: World-Class!, Outstanding!, Impressive!, Inspiring!, then book Chris Alexander to speak at your next meeting.

Because of Chris Alexander's books, powerful messages, and engaging humorous teaching gift, businesses and organizations throughout the world invite him to speak and coach their executives and business teams.

Executives from client companies such as The Irvine Company, Freedom Village, CAHSAH, Mercedes Benz, Interior Specialists, Inc., and Johnson & Johnson say that it is Alexander's 30 years of real world business experience, examples, and results that have struck a chord with them and won him rave reviews and acclaim.

Chris Alexander is an expert at building organizational culture, high-performance teamwork, and world-class customer service.

He conducts Synergy retreats, custom designed training workshops, and culture change programs in the following areas:

▶ Synergy Strategic Planning;

▶ Synergy World-Class Leadership;

▶ Synergy "WOW" Factor!;

▶ Synergy Team Power; and

▶ Synergy Sales Power.

Keynotes and speaking topics:

▶ Catch the Wind with Your Wings;

▶ Synergy "WOW" Factor!;

▶ Synergy World-Class Leadership;

▶ Synergy Strategic Leadership; and

▶ Synergy Team Power.

He says: "Synergy is about those magic moments–when working in concert toward a shared destiny–communication flows openly, and everyone feels a sense of belonging and connection. That synchronicity multiplies, energy, focus, fun, productivity and profits. We see it in sports teams and in business teams–there's no difference."

Chris Alexander is an example of the American dream: He was born in a small country in the middle of Africa, then called Rhodesia and now renamed Zimbabwe. He emigrated from Africa to the U.S. more than 20 years ago and is the author of *Catch the Wind with Your Wings, Creating Extraordinary Joy, Joy in the Workplace, Synergizing Your Business* - a series of 5 business books which includes his new book, *Synergy Team Power.*

He has also authored many successful business audios, CDs, and DVDs to support his training programs. Along with a team of educational specialists, Alexander won the prestigious *Los Angeles Area Emmy Award for Overall Excellence in Business Education for the Coast Telecourse, Dollar$ and Sense: Personal Finance for the 21st Century.* Alexander's largest audience is his two PBS TV shows, titled *Creating Extraordinary Joy* and *Joy in the Workplace*, which reaches 4.5 million people with each broadcast.

Alexander's stories, anecdotes, international experience, and fresh feet-on-the-ground examples will "WOW" your audiences . . . and like so many groups, you will want him to come back—again and again.

"I am enough of an artist to draw fully on my imagination. Imagination is more important than knowledge. Knowledge is limited. Imagination encircles the world."

-Albert Einstein

For more information:
(U.S.) 949/586-0511
TheTeam@SynergyTeamPower.com

Book orders:
Team@SynergyTeamPower.com

To book Alexander for your next event,
contact:
Maryna@SynergyTeamPower.com

Visit us on the web:
SynergyTeamPower.com
AlexanderSpeaks.com

Get Smart:

The 5 Success Habits
PERSONAL Goal Planner

*Write out a **PERSONAL** goal*
for each one of the Success Habits

Starting date:	_____/_____/_____
Achievement date:	_____/_____/_____
Building Trust	
Right Mental Attitude	
Make it Fun!	
Be a "First-Giver"	
Be a Synergist	